Better Homes and Gardens®

Oven Meals

On the cover: Plan a meal around *Oven-Baked Beef Stew* served over squares of corn bread. Then, end the meal with *Fruited Baked Apples* and cream. (See recipes, page 10.)

Above: Try this home-style meal tonight. The menu features *Chicken Fricassee* served with rice, *Scalloped Spinach*, and *Peaches 'n Cream Crisp* for dessert. (See recipes, page 17.)

Contents

BETTER HOMES AND GARDENS BOOKS

Editorial Director: Don Dooley
Managing Editor: Malcolm E. Robinson   Art Director: John Berg
Asst. Managing Editor: Lawrence D. Clayton   Asst. Art Director: Randall Yontz
Food Editor: Nancy Morton
Senior Food Editor: Joyce Trollope
Associate Editors: Sharyl Heiken, Rosemary C. Hutchinson
Assistant Editors: Catherine Penney, Elizabeth Walter, Sandra Mapes, Elizabeth Strait
Designers: Harijs Priekulis, Faith Berven

Our seal assures you that every recipe in *Oven Meals* is endorsed by the Better Homes and Gardens Test Kitchen. Each recipe is thoroughly tested for family appeal, practicality, and deliciousness.

Know your oven

Save time, money, and energy by preparing oven meals.* To use your oven to the best advantage, learn what you can and cannot do with your oven.

Save time by putting all the dishes for one meal in the oven and setting the timer. Fill the oven, even if this means baking something for tomorrow's meal. Then, you can leave to do something else.

A special time-saver is the oven with a time-controlled setting (sometimes referred to as programmed cooking). This oven feature frees you from the kitchen for even longer periods of time. Simply put the food into the oven when you have time, several hours ahead of serving, and take it out when you need it— cooked.

Types available include the cook-and-hold oven (food cooks and then keeps warm until serving); the delay-and-cook oven (food is placed in the unheated oven several hours before cooking begins); and the delay-cook-hold oven, which is a combination of the other two time-controlled ovens. All three types help greatly in time management for the homemaker.

Save money by using the less tender cuts of meat, which are usually less expensive. Long, slow cooking is just what these meat cuts need to make them tender and flavorful. By using the oven to cook the majority of the meal, you will also save energy, which in turn will save money.

Save energy by using your oven to capacity. Put as much of the meal as possible in the oven. Don't peek into the oven during cooking just to check on the dinner's progress— this causes a heat loss. Use the oven window if you have one. Also, preheat the oven only when necessary (see tip on page 42). Preheating too long wastes heat.

Bake foods only till done—excessive cooking not only overcooks the food, it also wastes energy. After cooking, when the oven has been turned off, slip leftovers, plates, or serving dishes into the oven for warming and make use of stored heat.

Also make sure that your range is well insulated and that the oven door fits tightly. If your oven door doesn't seal tightly, check with an appliance serviceman and have it adjusted.

Sometimes, low-voltage conditions occur during hot or cold weather spells or other times when the demand for power is great. You'll find that the warm-up time on a standard size electric oven probably will be affected and preheating time may take longer. But, since oven temperatures are controlled by a thermostat, if there is enough power available to reach the oven, the thermostat will cause the oven to cycle on and off, thus maintaining the proper temperature. Therefore, cooking times probably will not be affected.

However, when using portable heating appliances, such as a countertop oven, a power reduction can result in slower operation of the appliance. In fact, the heating elements may never reach the desired temperature and baking results may not be satisfactory during low-voltage conditions.

Check the oven temperature occasionally with an oven thermometer. If necessary, have the thermostat adjusted by a qualified serviceman.

Practice safety when working with your oven. Use dry potholders to remove hot dishes or oven racks—damp potholders will cause steam when in contact with the hot dish or rack and may burn your hands. Pull the oven rack out to a safe, locked position before removing heavy containers—you'll be less likely to touch the hot oven sides and you'll be in a better position to pick up the heavy container. When opening the oven door, let the blast of hot air escape before reaching into the hot oven. Remove covers of baking dishes away from you to avoid the steam. And teach children that the oven is hot and is *not* to be touched.

Read the use-and-care booklet to learn how to use your particular oven. Then, heed any warnings and instructions given. Be sure to keep the information in a place where you can refer to it often.

Learn where to place foods in the oven. Before you start the oven, adjust the racks. It's easier than trying to juggle hot oven racks. When only one rack is needed, place it so that the oven is divided in half. When using two racks, place them so that the oven is divided into thirds. Arrange pans so that they are staggered (see tip on page 67).

Choose appropriate baking containers, as specified in the recipes. When a baking *pan* is called for, you should use a metal container. Use a glass container when a baking *dish* is specified. And if you substitute a glass dish for a metal pan, be sure to *reduce* the oven temperature by 25°. Also, be sure that the dishes and casseroles you choose for baking are ovenproof.

Cleaning the oven is one task that can't be avoided. But today's special oven cleaners help speed up the process. If you are using one of these oven cleaners, carefully read and follow the directions on the label.

Automatically cleaned ovens are a boon to the modern homemaker. There are two types of automatic cleaning ovens on today's ranges. The first is the self-cleaning oven, in which soil is burned away at high temperatures. The other is the continuous cleaning oven, which has a specially treated coating on the oven surfaces. Consult your range's use-and-care booklet as to how to clean the oven.

Use countertop oven appliances whenever possible, if you have one. By using the small ovens, you won't have to heat up the large oven of the range, resulting in the use of less wattage and the saving of energy. Portable ovens also make it possible for you to cook wherever there is an electrical outlet. However, some appliances should not be used outdoors. Check the use-and-care booklet if this is in your plans.

Different countertop oven units do different jobs—some bake, roast, toast, and grill, others toast and bake, and still others only broil or only toast. If you plan to use your appliance for baking, make sure that it is designed for baking and is thermostatically controlled.

Here are some safety precautions you should keep in mind when using small portable ovens. Make sure that the appliance has a UL (Underwriters Laboratories) label attached. Keep the appliance clean to avoid a fire. Remove the cord from the outlet when cleaning, and always remove the cord from the wall by grasping the plug. Read the operating instructions carefully. Check out the wattage and amperage and don't overload the circuits. Avoid extension cords. During operation, be sure that the portable oven does not touch any flammable materials, such as curtains, and other items, such as plastic wrap and plastic dishes. Also, place the appliance at least one inch away from the wall.

Using a microwave oven is an efficient way to cook in terms of saving energy and time. This type of oven has a vacuum tube called a magnetron, which generates electromagnetic waves. The waves penetrate the food and cause the moisture molecules in the food to vibrate. This vibration causes friction, which in turn produces heat, and the heat causes the food to cook in a short time. Although cooking times are shortened with a microwave oven, you may have to stay close by to stir the food occasionally, thus assuring even doneness of the food.

Microwave ovens are safe to use, since manufacturers must comply with strict safety standards set by the government. However, you must make sure that the door seals are clean and in good condition and that objects are not closed in the door when the oven is in operation. Check the owner's manual regarding the care and upkeep of the oven.

Choosing utensils for use in a microwave oven is important. Ovenproof glass, glass ceramic, paper, and some plastics are all containers that can be used in most microwave ovens. However, check the instruction book that comes with your particular oven.

*An oven meal consists of two or three items (a main dish plus one or two more dishes) that are cooked in the oven.

All-Occasion Oven Meals

For family, or any special occasion, an oven meal is a boon to the busy homemaker. This make-ahead dinner includes Pizza Strata and Apricot-Pear Compote, both oven baked, accompanied by Italian green beans, Italian Salad Mold, and breadsticks. (See index for page numbers.)

Everyday family dinners

Make family mealtime exciting—inject interest in it with some of the delicious and nutritious menus featured in this section. And to minimize preparation time, take advantage of the preparation tips included with each menu.

FAMILY FARE

Ham Grab Bags

Hot Herb Rolls

Lettuce Wedge   French Dressing

Butterscotch Pudding

Beverage

Preparation tip: Prepare rolls. Use dough resting time to make and chill instant pudding. Shape rolls, then make grab bags while rolls rise. Bake rolls and grab bags together. When rolls finish baking, remove from oven and let them stand while grab bags finish baking.

Hot Herb Rolls

  2½ **cups packaged biscuit mix**
    1 **package active dry yeast**
    1 **tablespoon butter, softened**
    2 **teaspoons Italian salad dressing**
       mix

In bowl combine the biscuit mix and yeast. Add ⅔ cup warm water (110°). Beat vigorously ½ minute. Knead dough on floured surface till smooth, about 20 times. Let rest 10 minutes. Roll to 12x9-inch rectangle. Spread with butter; sprinkle salad dressing mix over dough. Cut dough into twelve 3-inch squares. Roll up jelly-roll fashion; place, seam side down, on lightly greased baking sheet. Make slits in rolls ½ inch apart and halfway through dough. Curve rolls slightly to separate slits. Cover; let rise till double (about 40 minutes). Bake at 400° till golden, 10 to 15 minutes. Serve warm. Makes 12 rolls.

Ham Grab Bags

    1 **18-ounce can sweet potatoes**
    1 **8-ounce can whole cranberry sauce**
  ½ **teaspoon Dijon-style mustard**
    1 **20-ounce can pie-sliced apples,**
       drained
  ¼ **cup packed brown sugar (optional)**
       • • •
  ¼ **cup butter** *or* **margarine, softened**
    1 **tablespoon snipped parsley**
  ¼ **teaspoon grated lemon peel**
    1 **tablespoon lemon juice**
    1 **16-ounce package ham steaks (8**
       slices)
    1 **16-ounce can cut Italian green**
       beans, drained

Drain sweet potatoes, reserving 1 tablespoon of the syrup; slice potatoes and set aside. In a bowl combine the cranberry sauce, reserved sweet potato syrup, and mustard; set aside. If desired, sprinkle apple slices and sweet potatoes with brown sugar; set aside. In a bowl combine the softened butter, parsley, lemon peel, lemon juice, and dash pepper; set aside. On four 18-inch lengths of heavy foil, layer *half* the ham slices, sweet potatoes, beans, apple slices, and cranberry mixture. Dot with lemon-butter mixture. Repeat layers. Or, roll the ham slices around fruit and vegetable mixture. (If desired, use only the cranberry mixture or lemon-butter.) Seal foil pouches loosely. Place on baking sheet. Bake at 400° till heated through, 25 to 30 minutes. Makes 4 servings.

You will win praise from family members when you serve a meal centered around *Ham Grab Bags*. Each serving of this tart, tempting main dish bakes in its own foil pouch.

CHILLY NIGHT DINNER

Oven-Baked Beef Stew
Corn Bread
Cottage-Peach Mold
Celery Sticks
Fruited Baked Apples   Cream
Beverage

Preparation tip: *Make and refrigerate the molded salad ahead so it can chill at least 5 hours—overnight is better. Synchronize baking the stew, apples, and corn bread. Place stew and apples in oven 2¼ hours before dinner. After 1 hour, stir the vegetables and thickening into stew. Test apples. If done, take them out to cool. If not done, give them another 15 minutes. Prepare corn bread so it bakes just 30 minutes before serving time.*

Cottage-Peach Mold

A fancy fix-up for peaches and cottage cheese—

⅓ **cup sugar**
2 **envelopes unflavored gelatin**
¼ **teaspoon ground ginger**
    Dash salt
• • •
1 **30-ounce can peach slices**
2 **tablespoons lemon juice**
1½ **cups cream-style cottage cheese**
    Lettuce

In a medium saucepan combine sugar, gelatin, ginger, and salt. Drain peaches, reserving the syrup. Add enough water to reserved syrup to measure 2¼ cups liquid. Stir liquid into gelatin mixture. Stir over low heat till gelatin and sugar are dissolved. Remove from heat. Place the drained peaches and lemon juice in a blender container. Puree the peaches till smooth. Stir peaches into gelatin mixture till thoroughly combined. Chill till partially set. Fold in the cottage cheese. Turn gelatin mixture into a 6-cup mold. Chill 5 to 6 hours or overnight. Unmold the salad onto a lettuce-lined plate. Makes 8 servings.

Oven-Baked Beef Stew

This robust stew is shown on the cover—

½ **cup all-purpose flour**
2 **pounds beef stew meat**
3 **tablespoons shortening**
1 **16-ounce can tomatoes**
5 **carrots, cut in 1-inch pieces**
½ **cup chopped onion**
¼ **cup chopped celery**
¼ **cup chili sauce**
1 **tablespoon instant beef bouillon granules**
1 **10-ounce package frozen Mexican-style vegetables**
1 **16-ounce can cut green beans, drained**
1 **10-ounce package corn bread mix**

Combine ¼ cup of the flour, ¼ teaspoon salt, and ⅛ teaspoon pepper. Add to meat, tossing to coat. In skillet brown the meat in hot shortening; transfer to 3-quart casserole. Drain off ½ cup liquid from tomatoes, reserving liquid; cut up tomatoes. Add tomatoes and remaining liquid, carrots, onion, celery, chili sauce, and bouillon granules. Mix well.

Cover tightly and bake at 325° for 1 hour. Combine remaining ¼ cup flour with reserved tomato liquid; stir into stew along with Mexican-style vegetables and green beans. Cover and bake for 1¼ hours longer.

Prepare corn bread, following package directions. Bake in greased 8x8x2-inch baking dish at 325° for 25 to 30 minutes. Cool slightly; cut into squares. To serve, spoon stew over corn bread. Serves 6 to 8.

Fruited Baked Apples

Core 6 large baking apples (do not cut all the way through). Peel strip from top of each. Place apples in 11x7½x1½-inch baking pan. Combine 1 large banana, chopped; 1 cup cranberries, chopped; ½ cup sugar; ½ teaspoon ground cinnamon; and ¼ teaspoon vanilla. Fill apples with mixture. Sprinkle with ¼ cup chopped nuts. Combine ½ cup cranberry juice cocktail and excess filling; pour mixture around apples. Bake at 325° for 1 to 1¼ hours. Spoon syrup over. Serves 6.

Preparation tip: *For those days when you are short on time, have this meal oven-ready to avoid rushing. Prepare the strata, salad, and compote ahead and refrigerate them. When you're ready to start dinner, place the strata and compote in the oven. When the compote is finished baking, remove it to a cooling rack. Continue baking the strata. Prepare the green beans, unmold the salad, and dinner is ready.*

Italian Salad Mold

If desired, reserve some clear gelatin and zucchini to make a fancy crown for this salad—

>   2 3-ounce packages lemon-flavored
>   gelatin
> ½ envelope Italian salad dressing
>   mix
> 1½ cups boiling water
>   2 cups cold water
> ¼ cup vinegar
>   • • •
>   1 cup chopped lettuce
>   1 cup quartered and thinly
>   sliced zucchini
> ½ cup shredded carrot
> ¼ cup sliced radishes
>   Lettuce
>   Mayonnaise *or* salad dressing

In bowl combine gelatin and salad dressing mix. Add boiling water; stir till gelatin is dissolved. Stir in cold water and vinegar. Chill till partially set. Fold the next four ingredients into gelatin. Pour mixture into 5½-cup mold. Chill till firm. Unmold on a lettuce-lined plate. Serve with mayonnaise or salad dressing. Makes 6 to 8 servings.

Pizza Strata

Zesty Italian dish pictured on pages 6 and 7—

>   8 slices white bread
>   1 pound Italian sausage
> ½ cup chopped onion
>   4 ounces sliced mozzarella cheese
>   1 8-ounce can pizza sauce
>   3 beaten eggs
> 1¾ cups milk
>   1 tablespoon snipped parsley
> ½ teaspoon dried oregano, crushed
> ¼ cup grated Parmesan cheese

Remove the crusts from *4 slices* of the bread; reserve crusts. Use remaining 4 slices of bread and crusts to cover the bottom of a greased 8x8x2-inch baking dish. In skillet cook sausage and onion till sausage is brown, about 10 minutes. Drain thoroughly. Spread meat-onion mixture over bread in baking dish. Cover meat with sliced mozzarella cheese. Spread pizza sauce over cheese. Cut the remaining 4 slices of trimmed bread on the diagonal; place in two rows atop sauce. (Bases should overlap points of preceding triangles.) Combine eggs, milk, parsley, and oregano. Pour over bread. Cover tightly; chill at least 1 hour or overnight. Bake, covered, at 325° for 30 minutes. Uncover; bake 30 minutes longer. Sprinkle with Parmesan cheese. Continue baking till firm, 10 to 15 minutes longer. Let stand 5 to 10 minutes before serving. Cut the strata into squares. Makes 6 servings.

Apricot-Pear Compote

If desired, replace liqueur with orange juice—

>   1 29-ounce can pear slices
> ½ cup dried apricots, halved
> ¼ cup sugar
> ¼ cup orange juice
> ¼ cup sliced maraschino cherries
>   2 tablespoons orange liqueur
> ⅛ teaspoon ground nutmeg

In a 1½-quart casserole combine all ingredients. Cover and chill in the refrigerator at least 1 hour or overnight. Bake, covered, at 325° till apricots are tender, 50 to 60 minutes. Serve warm or cool. Makes 6 servings.

OLD-FASHIONED DINNER

Vegetable-Topped Rump Roast
Muffins   Butter
Frozen Spiced Peach Salad
Apple Dessert Bake
Beverage

Preparation tip: Prepare roast and put into oven. Make the dessert and add it to oven when vegetables are added to the roast. Remove dessert when done and continue cooking meat and vegetables till tender.

Apple Dessert Bake

½ cup dark corn syrup
⅓ cup water
1 tablespoon lemon juice
1 teaspoon ground cinnamon
½ teaspoon ground nutmeg
4 tart medium apples, peeled, cored, and sliced
1 cup all-purpose flour
½ cup sugar
1½ teaspoons baking powder
⅔ cup milk
¼ cup shortening
½ teaspoon vanilla

In saucepan combine first 5 ingredients. Add apples. Cover; bring to boiling. Remove from heat. Meanwhile, in a bowl stir together flour, sugar, baking powder, and ½ teaspoon salt. Add milk, shortening, and vanilla; beat till smooth. Pour hot apple mixture into 10x6x2-inch baking dish. Immediately pour batter over apple mixture. Bake at 325° till topping is done, 30 to 35 minutes. Serve warm with cream, if desired. Serves 6 to 8.

◀ **Your family is sure to enjoy** a dinner featuring *Vegetable-Topped Rump Roast.* Add a chilly frozen salad to your piping hot oven meal for a contrast in food temperatures.

Vegetable-Topped Rump Roast

2 tablespoons all-purpose flour
½ teaspoon salt
¼ teaspoon paprika
    Dash pepper
1 2-pound boneless beef round rump roast (rolled and tied)
2 tablespoons cooking oil
1 11½-ounce can condensed bean with bacon soup
1 teaspoon beef-flavored gravy base
1 bay leaf
12 small onions, peeled (1 pound)
6 medium carrots, halved (1 pound)
1 medium green pepper, cut in pieces

Combine first 4 ingredients; coat roast with mixture. In Dutch oven brown the roast on all sides in hot oil. Remove from heat. Combine soup, gravy base, bay leaf, and ½ cup water; pour over roast. Cook, covered, at 325° for 1½ hours, stirring soup mixture occasionally. Add onions, carrots, and green pepper. Cook till meat and vegetables are tender, about 1 hour longer. To serve, discard bay leaf and remove strings from meat. Arrange meat and vegetables on platter. Spoon some soup mixture atop; pass remaining mixture. Serves 6.

Frozen Spiced Peach Salad

1 5⅓-ounce can evaporated milk
1 30-ounce jar spiced peaches
1 3-ounce package cream cheese, softened
¼ cup sugar
1 tablespoon lemon juice
1 cup tiny marshmallows
½ cup chopped pecans

Freeze evaporated milk in refrigerator tray till crystals form around edge. Drain peaches, reserving ½ cup syrup. Finely chop the peaches, discarding pits. In bowl beat cream cheese and sugar together till smooth. Gradually beat in reserved syrup and lemon juice. Fold in peaches, marshmallows, and nuts. Whip icy-cold milk till stiff. Fold whipped milk into cheese mixture. Turn into 11x7½x1½-inch pan. Freeze till firm. Serves 8.

WHEN THE BUDGET IS TIGHT

Hawaiian Beef Loaves *or*
Beef Wellington Loaves
Oven Rice
Buttered Carrots
Zucchini Salad
Radishes and Celery Sticks
Spicy Marble Squares
Beverage

Preparation tip: *Plan baking time around the meat loaf you choose. Wellington loaves bake about 1¼ hours, while the Hawaiian loaves bake about 1 hour. The rice takes only 1 hour; stir halfway through baking. Broil cake topping just before serving.*

Beef Wellington Loaves

 2 beaten eggs
 2 10¾-ounce cans condensed
      golden mushroom soup
 ½ cup fine dry bread crumbs
 ½ cup finely chopped onion
 1 teaspoon salt
 ¼ teaspoon pepper
 2 pounds lean ground beef
 1 package refrigerated crescent rolls
      (8 rolls)
 1 cup water
 2 tablespoons snipped parsley

In mixing bowl combine eggs, ½ *cup* of the soup, crumbs, onion, salt, and pepper. Add ground meat; mix well. Shape mixture into two 6x3-inch loaves and place in shallow baking pan. Bake at 350° for 55 to 60 minutes. Spoon off drippings from meat. Separate crescent rolls into 4 rectangles; seal perforations. Place 2 rectangles of dough crosswise over tops and down sides of each loaf, overlapping slightly. Bake till dough is golden, 15 to 20 minutes longer. In small saucepan combine remaining soup, water, and snipped parsley; heat to bubbling. Pass sauce with loaves and rice. Makes 8 servings.

Oven Rice

 1 cup long grain rice
 2¼ cups water
 1 teaspoon salt

Place uncooked rice in 1½-quart casserole. Add water and salt. Cover and bake at 350° till rice is tender, about 1 hour. Fluff rice once with a fork about halfway through cooking. Makes 8 servings.

Spicy Marble Squares

 ¾ cup granulated sugar
 ½ cup shortening
 1 egg
 2 cups all-purpose flour
 2 teaspoons baking powder
 ½ teaspoon salt
 ¾ cup milk
 2 tablespoons light molasses
 ½ teaspoon ground cinnamon
 ¼ teaspoon ground nutmeg
 ⅛ teaspoon ground cloves
 6 tablespoons butter *or* margarine,
      softened
 ½ cup packed brown sugar
 3 tablespoons milk
 ⅔ cup flaked coconut
 2 ripe bananas

In mixing bowl cream together the granulated sugar and shortening. Add egg; beat well. Stir together thoroughly the flour, baking powder, and salt. Add to creamed mixture alternately with the ¾ cup milk, beating well after each addition. Divide batter in half. To one half add the molasses, cinnamon, nutmeg, and cloves; mix well. Spoon spiced and plain batters alternately into greased 9x9x2-inch baking pan. Zigzag spatula through batter to marble. Bake at 350° till cake tests done, 35 to 40 minutes. In mixing bowl combine softened butter or margarine, brown sugar, and the 3 tablespoons milk; stir in flaked coconut. Set aside. Slice bananas diagonally in ¼-inch-thick slices. Arrange in a single layer atop warm cake. Spoon coconut mixture over bananas, spreading evenly. Broil 3 to 4 inches from heat for 3 to 4 minutes. Serves 8 or 9.

Give character to meat loaves—feature a Hawaiian theme when serving the *Hawaiian Beef Loaves*. The typical sweet and sour sauce makes this meat loaf extra tangy. Set the table with brightly colored linens and pour a frosty beverage in coconut shells.

Hawaiian Beef Loaves

In a large mixing bowl blend 1 envelope brown gravy mix and ½ cup milk. Stir in 1 teaspoon instant minced onion; let mixture stand a few minutes. Stir 2 beaten eggs, 1 tablespoon snipped parsley, 2 teaspoons soy sauce, ½ teaspoon salt, and dash pepper into gravy mixture. Stir in 1 cup soft bread crumbs. Add 2 pounds ground beef; mix well to combine all ingredients.

Shape the meat mixture into 2 loaves; place the beef loaves in a shallow baking pan. Bake at 350° for 50 minutes. Spoon off the excess fat. Using one 16-ounce can sweet-sour sauce, pour a small amount of the sweet-sour sauce over the beef loaves. Return to oven and bake 15 minutes longer. Heat remaining sweet-sour sauce. Serve sauce with meat loaves and rice. Makes 8 servings.

Zucchini Salad

    4 small zucchini, thinly sliced
    4 tomatoes, cut in wedges
    1 small green pepper, cut in strips
 ¼ cup chopped green onion
 ¼ cup snipped parsley
 ¾ cup salad oil
 ¼ cup vinegar
    1 small clove garlic, minced
 ½ teaspoon salt
    Lettuce

In bowl combine zucchini, tomatoes, green pepper, onion, and parsley. Stir together the oil, vinegar, garlic, salt, and dash pepper. Pour mixture over vegetables. Chill several hours. Drain off marinade. Serve salad in lettuce-lined bowl. Sprinkle with additional salt and freshly ground pepper. Serves 8 to 10.

LOW-CALORIE DINNER

Tomato Juice
Flounder Continental
Fruity Beet Bake
Breadsticks
Lettuce   Low-Calorie Dressing
Rice Meringue Pudding
Beverage

Preparation tip: *To speed up preparation time cook rice for the pudding ahead. Now, the meal can be ready in less than 1 hour. Assembling the fish, beets, and dessert will take you 30 minutes. Allow another 25 minutes for baking time. Remove pudding from the oven when golden and serve warm.*

Rice Meringue Pudding

A luscious 150 calories per serving—

  ⅓ **cup long grain rice**
  2 **beaten egg yolks**
  1 **egg white**
  1 **cup skim milk**
  2 **tablespoons sugar**
  2 **tablespoons water**
  ⅛ **teaspoon ground cinnamon**
  ½ **teaspoon vanilla**
  1 **egg white**
    Few drops almond extract
  1 **tablespoon sugar**

Cook rice according to package directions; set aside. Meanwhile, in small, heavy saucepan combine egg yolks, 1 egg white, milk, the 2 tablespoons sugar, water, and cinnamon. Cook and stir over medium-low heat till mixture is slightly thickened and coats a metal spoon, 10 to 12 minutes. Remove from heat. Stir in vanilla and cooked rice. Turn into a 1-quart casserole. Beat 1 egg white and almond extract till soft peaks form. Gradually add the 1 tablespoon sugar. Beat till stiff peaks form. Drop egg white mixture in four dollops atop pudding. Bake at 325° till meringue is golden, 12 to 15 minutes. Makes 4 servings.

Flounder Continental

Enjoy a creamy sauce atop fish fillets. This one is a delicious 160 calories per serving—

  4 **small fresh *or* frozen flounder,
      haddock, *or* sole fillets
      (1 pound)**
  1 **cup sliced fresh mushrooms**
  ¼ **cup chopped onion**
  1 **tablespoon butter *or* margarine**
      • • •
  2 **tablespoons all-purpose flour**
  ½ **teaspoon instant chicken bouillon
      granules**
  ¼ **teaspoon seasoned salt**
  1 **cup skim milk**
    Salt
  1 **teaspoon lemon juice**
  1 **tablespoon snipped parsley**

Thaw frozen fillets. In saucepan cook the mushrooms and onion in butter till tender but not brown. Stir in the flour, chicken bouillon granules, and seasoned salt. Stir in the milk all at once; cook and stir till mixture is thickened and bubbly.

Place the fish fillets in a single layer in 11x7½x1½-inch baking pan; sprinkle fish lightly with salt and drizzle with the lemon juice. Spoon the mushroom mixture atop fish. Cover and bake at 325° till fish flakes easily when tested with a fork, about 25 minutes. Transfer fish to a serving platter. Sprinkle with snipped parsley. Makes 4 servings.

Fruity Beet Bake

Only 50 skinny calories per serving—

  1 **16-ounce can *or* jar sliced beets,
      drained**
  ½ **cup low-calorie apricot preserves**
  2 **teaspoons lemon juice**
  ⅛ **teaspoon salt**
    Dash ground cloves

Place beets in a 2-cup baking dish. In a bowl stir together the apricot preserves, lemon juice, salt, and cloves; spoon over beets. Bake, uncovered, at 325° till beets are heated, about 25 minutes. Stir beets and glaze together before serving. Makes 4 servings.

HOME-STYLE FAVORITE

Chicken Fricassee
Scalloped Spinach
Rice
Crisp Relish Assortment
Spiced Apple Rings
Peaches 'n Cream Crisp
Beverage

Preparation tip: *One hour before serving, place the chicken and dessert in oven to bake. Meanwhile, prepare the spinach casserole. After 30 minutes of baking time, remove the dessert and bake spinach casserole. Bake 25 minutes, then add the crumb topping to spinach casserole. Continue baking the chicken and spinach casseroles till done.*

Scalloped Spinach

Cheese and onion team up to complement the flavor of the chopped spinach—

> 2 10-ounce packages frozen
>   chopped spinach
> ¾ cup milk
> ¾ cup shredded American cheese
>   (3 ounces)
> 3 beaten eggs
> 3 tablespoons chopped onion
> ½ teaspoon salt
>   Dash pepper
> 1 cup coarse soft bread crumbs
> 1 tablespoon butter *or* margarine,
>   melted

Cook spinach according to package directions; drain well. Mix with milk, ½ *cup* of the cheese, beaten eggs, chopped onion, salt, and pepper. Turn mixture into a greased 8x8x2-inch baking pan. Bake at 350° for 25 minutes.

Combine the soft bread crumbs, remaining shredded cheese, and melted butter or margarine; sprinkle atop spinach. Bake till a knife inserted off-center comes out clean, 10 to 15 minutes longer. Let spinach stand 5 minutes before serving. Makes 6 servings.

Chicken Fricassee

This all-time favorite is shown on page 2—

> 1 3- to 4-pound ready-to-cook fryer
>   chicken, cut in serving-size
>   pieces
> ½ cup all-purpose flour
> 1 teaspoon salt
> ⅛ teaspoon pepper
> ¼ cup shortening
>   • • •
> ½ cup chopped celery
> ¼ cup chopped onion
>   • • •
> 1 10½-ounce can condensed cream of
>   mushroom soup
> ¾ cup water
> 2 tablespoons chopped canned pimiento

Coat chicken pieces with a mixture of the flour, salt, and pepper. In skillet brown the chicken in hot shortening. Transfer browned chicken to a 3-quart casserole. Cook chopped celery and onion in same skillet till tender but not brown. Drain off excess fat. Stir in the cream of mushroom soup, water, and chopped pimiento. Pour soup mixture over chicken in casserole. Cover and bake at 350° till chicken is tender, about 1 hour. Serve chicken and sauce with rice. Makes 6 servings.

Peaches 'n Cream Crisp

Enhance canned peach slices with the natural flavors of oats and sweet brown sugar—

> 1 29-ounce can peach slices,
>   drained
>   • • •
> ¾ cup quick-cooking rolled oats
> ½ cup packed brown sugar
> ½ cup all-purpose flour
> 6 tablespoons butter *or* margarine
>   • • •
>   Vanilla ice cream

Place drained peach slices in a single layer in 8x1½-inch round baking dish. Combine the rolled oats, brown sugar, flour, and butter. Sprinkle mixture over peaches. Bake at 350° till topping is crisp, about 30 minutes. Serve warm with ice cream. Makes 6 servings.

NOVEMBER FEAST

Cran-Rice Stuffed Cornish Hens
Baked Asparagus
Cheesy Corn Bread
Frosted Pear-Avocado Salad
Celery Sticks
Chocolate Pudding Especial
Beverage

Preparation tip: *Make and chill dessert and salad. Allow 1½ hours to roast hens. Add asparagus 45 minutes before dinner and corn bread 30 minutes before dinner.*

Cheesy Corn Bread

¼ **cup finely chopped onion**
1 **tablespoon butter** *or* **margarine**
1 **10-ounce package corn bread mix**
½ **cup shredded sharp American cheese (2 ounces)**

In a skillet cook onion in butter or margarine till tender but not brown. Prepare corn bread mix according to package directions. Stir in the cooked onion and shredded cheese. Turn batter into greased 8x8x2-inch baking pan. Bake at 375° till done, about 30 minutes. Remove from oven; keep corn bread warm. (If necessary, reheat corn bread in baking pan covered with foil.) Before serving, cut corn bread into squares. Makes 9 servings.

On a cold, November day—any day for that matter—your family is sure to enjoy tender *Cran-Rice Stuffed Cornish Hens.* And don't forget to pass the butter to melt over squares of warmed and mellow *Cheesy Corn Bread,* doubly flavored with cheese and onion.

Cran-Rice Stuffed Cornish Hens

⅔ cup long grain rice
3 tablespoons butter *or* margarine
2 cups water
2 teaspoons instant chicken bouillon
    granules
¾ cup chopped fresh cranberries
3 tablespoons sugar
1 teaspoon grated orange peel
2 tablespoons orange juice
4 1-pound ready-to-cook Rock Cornish
    game hens
Orange Glaze

In saucepan cook rice in butter for 5 minutes, stirring frequently. Stir in water and chicken bouillon granules. Bring mixture to boiling. Reduce heat. Cook, covered, over low heat till rice is tender, about 20 minutes. Stir in the cranberries, sugar, orange peel, and orange juice. Salt cavity of birds. Stuff each with cranberry mixture; push drumsticks under band of skin at tail or tie to tail. Place birds on rack in shallow roasting pan. Cover the hens loosely with foil and roast at 375° for 30 minutes. Uncover and continue to roast 1 hour longer, brushing occasionally with Orange Glaze. Makes 4 servings.

Orange Glaze: Combine ¼ cup orange juice and 3 tablespoons butter, melted.

Chocolate Pudding Especial

12 regular marshmallows
⅓ cup milk
½ cup broken milk chocolate bars with
    almonds (2½ ounces)
½ cup whipping cream
¼ cup coarsely crushed vanilla wafers
1 tablespoon butter, melted

In small saucepan combine marshmallows and milk; stir over medium heat till marshmallows are melted. Remove from heat. Add chocolate to marshmallow mixture, stirring till chocolate is melted. Cool. Whip cream; fold into chocolate mixture. Combine the vanilla wafers and melted butter. Spoon chocolate mixture into 4 sherbet glasses. Top with the crumb mixture. Chill 3 to 4 hours. Serves 4.

Vegetable cooking tip

Oven-cook a block of frozen vegetables in a tightly covered casserole. Top with 1 or 2 tablespoons butter; season with salt and pepper. (If cooking lima beans, add 2 tablespoons water.) Although cooking times for individual vegetables vary, allow about 60 minutes for vegetables at 325°; 50 minutes for those at 350°; and 45 minutes for vegetables at 375°. Then, test for doneness, and if needed, cook 5 to 10 minutes longer. Stir the vegetables occasionally after the first 20 minutes and stir again just before serving.

Frosted Pear-Avocado Salad

1 16-ounce can pear halves
1 tablespoon vinegar
1 3-ounce package lime-flavored
    gelatin
1 3-ounce package cream cheese
1 medium avocado, pitted, peeled,
    and diced (1 cup)

Drain pears, reserving syrup. Dice pears; set aside. Add water to syrup to make 1¾ cups. Heat syrup mixture, vinegar, and ¼ teaspoon salt to boiling. Stir in gelatin till dissolved. Soften cream cheese. Gradually add ⅓ cup hot gelatin to cream cheese; beat till smooth. Pour gelatin-cheese mixture into 4-cup mold; chill till almost firm. Chill remaining gelatin till partially set. Fold in avocado and pears. Spoon over cheese layer. Chill till firm. Serves 4 to 6.

Baked Asparagus

1 10-ounce package frozen cut
    asparagus
1 to 2 tablespoons butter *or* margarine

Place cut asparagus in 1-quart casserole. Top with butter or margarine. Season with salt and pepper. Cover tightly. Bake at 375° for 45 minutes, stirring occasionally after 20 minutes. Stir again just before serving. Serves 4.

Meals for entertaining

When entertaining, a hostess can't be bothered with pot watching. So, prepare whole meals in the oven and have everything ready at one time. The menus in this section will give you more time with your guests.

COMMITTEE MEETING LUNCH

Velvety Chicken Casserole
Crescent Rolls   Butter
Fruit Pickles
Lemon-Macaroon Soufflés
Beverage

Preparation tip: *Press cookies into soufflé dishes in advance. Bake casserole. Meanwhile, finish making the soufflés. Bake soufflés while you eat the main course.*

Velvety Chicken Casserole

> 2 9-ounce packages frozen artichoke
>   hearts
> 1½ cups sliced fresh mushrooms
> 3 tablespoons butter *or* margarine
> 2 cups cubed cooked chicken
> 1 envelope chicken gravy mix
> 1 cup diced Swiss cheese
> ⅛ teaspoon dried marjoram, crushed
> 1 tablespoon dry sherry
> ½ cup soft bread crumbs
> 1 tablespoon snipped parsley

Cook artichokes, following package directions; drain. Cook mushrooms in *2 tablespoons* butter till tender. Place artichokes, mushrooms, and chicken in 2-quart baking dish. Prepare gravy mix, following package directions. Stir in cheese and marjoram till cheese melts. Stir in wine. Pour over chicken. Melt remaining butter; toss with crumbs. Sprinkle atop. Bake, uncovered, at 350° about 40 minutes. Trim with parsley. Serves 6.

Lemon-Macaroon Soufflés

> 6 soft coconut macaroons
> 6 teaspoons orange liqueur
> 6 beaten egg yolks
> 6 tablespoons butter, softened
> ⅓ cup granulated sugar
> ½ teaspoon grated lemon peel
> ¼ cup lemon juice
> 6 egg whites
> ⅓ cup granulated sugar
>   Powdered sugar

Place 1 coconut macaroon in *each* of six 1-cup soufflé dishes or 10-ounce glass baking dishes. Press cookie to fit bottom of dish. Sprinkle *each* macaroon with 1 teaspoon of the orange liqueur. Set dishes aside.

In small, heavy saucepan combine egg yolks, softened butter, ⅓ cup granulated sugar, lemon peel, lemon juice, and dash salt. Cook over low heat, stirring constantly, till slightly thickened. Remove from heat and beat well, about 2 minutes; set aside.

Beat egg whites till soft peaks form. Gradually add ⅓ cup sugar; beat till stiff peaks form. Fold yolk mixture into egg whites till blended. Spoon over macaroons in soufflé dishes or baking dishes. Place in shallow baking pan; pour boiling water around dishes to depth of ½ inch. Bake at 350° till tops spring back when touched lightly, 30 to 35 minutes. Sprinkle tops with sifted powdered sugar. Serve immediately. Makes 6 servings.

When the committee meeting convenes at ▶ your house, serve lunch on the patio. Team *Velvety Chicken Casserole* with fruit pickles, a basket of warm crescent rolls, and dessert for a guest-pleasing light meal.

BRUNCH FOR SIX

Broccoli-Egg Bake
French Breakfast Puffs *with*
Butter Balls
Honeyed Pear Ambrosia
Beverage

Preparation tip: *Make and chill dessert ahead of time. Bake casserole and muffins together, but remove muffins 5 minutes before casserole to sugar-coat tops.*

Broccoli-Egg Bake

      6 hard-cooked eggs
  ½ cup finely chopped fully cooked ham
      2 tablespoons butter *or* margarine,
          softened
      1 tablespoon finely chopped onion
  ½ teaspoon Worcestershire sauce
  ¼ teaspoon dry mustard
      2 10-ounce packages frozen broccoli
          spears, cooked and drained
  ¼ cup butter *or* margarine
  ¼ cup all-purpose flour
  2½ cups milk
      1 cup shredded sharp American cheese
          (4 ounces)
  1½ cups soft bread crumbs
  ¼ cup butter *or* margarine, melted

Halve eggs. Remove egg yolks; set egg whites aside. Mash yolks; stir in ham, 2 tablespoons softened butter, onion, Worcestershire sauce, and mustard. Fill egg whites with yolk mixture. Arrange cooked broccoli spears in bottom of a 12x7½x2-inch baking dish; place filled eggs on top. In saucepan melt ¼ cup butter; blend in flour and ¼ teaspoon salt. Stir in milk; cook quickly, stirring constantly, till mixture thickens and bubbles. Add cheese; stir till melted. Pour sauce over broccoli and eggs. Combine bread crumbs and ¼ cup melted butter; sprinkle over casserole. Bake at 350° till mixture is heated through, about 25 minutes. Makes 6 servings.

French Breakfast Puffs

Serve these delicate sugar-cinnamon topped muffins with butter balls —

  ½ cup sugar
  ⅓ cup shortening
      1 egg
  1½ cups all-purpose flour
  1½ teaspoons baking powder
  ½ teaspoon salt
  ¼ teaspoon ground nutmeg
          • • •
  ½ cup milk
  ½ cup sugar
      1 teaspoon ground cinnamon
      6 tablespoons butter *or* margarine,
          melted

In mixing bowl cream together the ½ cup sugar, shortening, and the egg. Stir together thoroughly the flour, baking powder, salt, and nutmeg; add to the creamed mixture alternately with milk, beating well after each addition. Fill 12 greased 2½-inch muffin pans ⅔ full with batter. Bake at 350° till done, 20 minutes. Combine the remaining ½ cup sugar and the cinnamon. Remove muffins from oven; immediately dip the muffin tops in melted butter, then in the cinnamon-sugar mixture till coated. Serve warm. Makes 12 muffins.

Honeyed Pear Ambrosia

Serve as the appetizer or the dessert —

      2 16-ounce cans pear halves
          (juice pack)
      1 11-ounce can mandarin orange
          sections, drained
  ¼ cup sliced maraschino cherries
      2 tablespoons honey
      2 tablespoons lime juice
      2 tablespoons shredded coconut,
          toasted

Drain pears and reserve the juice. In a compote combine drained pears, mandarin orange sections, and maraschino cherries. Combine the reserved pear juice, honey, and lime juice. Pour over fruit and stir carefully. Chill thoroughly, about 2 hours. Before serving, sprinkle toasted coconut over the top. Serves 6.

Preparation tip: *Give the beef rolls a head start in cooking while you prepare the potatoes. Make the gravy for the meat and arrange garnishes while the potatoes finish cooking.*

Potato Puff

**Packaged instant mashed potatoes
   (enough for 4 servings)**
½ cup light cream
2 tablespoons grated Parmesan cheese
1 teaspoon instant minced onion
½ teaspoon salt
• • •
3 egg yolks
3 stiffly beaten egg whites

Prepare potatoes according to package directions. Stir in cream; continue stirring over low heat till very hot. Add cheese, instant minced onion, and salt; mix well. Add egg yolks, one at a time, *beating well after each addition.* Add a little of the hot mixture to stiffly beaten egg whites; fold egg whites into potato mixture. Turn into ungreased 1½-quart casserole. Bake at 350° till knife inserted just off-center comes out clean, about 40 minutes. Serves 6.

Asparagus-Tomato Vinaigrette

Cook two 10-ounce packages frozen asparagus spears according to package directions. Chill. Cut 12 cherry tomatoes in half; combine with ½ cup Italian salad dressing in saucepan. Heat. Spoon tomatoes and hot dressing over asparagus; serve at once. Serves 6.

Crab-Stuffed Roulades of Beef

**2 pounds beef top round steak,
   cut ¼ inch thick**
1 beaten egg
¼ cup milk
1 tablespoon lemon juice
½ teaspoon Worcestershire sauce
¼ teaspoon salt
**1 7½-ounce can crab meat, drained,
   flaked, and cartilage removed**
½ cup fine dry bread crumbs
2 tablespoons snipped parsley
3 tablespoons cooking oil
¾ cup dry white wine
¾ cup water
**1 teaspoon instant beef bouillon
   granules**
1 clove garlic, minced
1 bay leaf
½ teaspoon salt
2 tablespoons cold water
2 tablespoons cornstarch

Cut beef into 12 rectangles; pound to ⅛-inch thickness. Combine egg, milk, lemon juice, Worcestershire, and ¼ teaspoon salt. Add crab meat, bread crumbs, and *1 tablespoon* of the parsley; mix thoroughly.

Place a heaping tablespoon of the filling at one end of each piece of meat; roll up. Secure with wooden picks. Heat oil in skillet. Brown part of the rolls at a time on all sides; transfer to 11x7½x1½-inch baking pan. Repeat with remaining rolls. To juices in skillet stir in wine, ¾ cup water, bouillon granules, garlic, bay leaf, remaining parsley, and ½ teaspoon salt. Bring to boiling, scraping pan to mix in crusty bits. Pour liquid over beef rolls in baking pan. Cover tightly with foil. Bake at 350° till tender, about 1 hour.

Transfer beef rolls to serving platter; keep hot. Strain pan juices into large measuring cup. Skim off excess fat. Add water, if necessary, to make 1½ cups. Pour juices into small saucepan. Stir in 2 to 3 tablespoons additional dry white wine, if desired. Stir the 2 tablespoons cold water into cornstarch. Add to pan juices; cook and stir till mixture thickens and bubbles. Pour some sauce over beef rolls and pass remainder. Garnish with additional parsley, if desired. Makes 6 servings.

One baking pan is all this main dish requires. The *Savory Ham Supper* combines ham with acorn squash, apples, and a cranberry glaze to provide a delicious and colorful meal. Expect compliments from your guests or family anytime you serve it.

DINNER FOR FRIENDS

Fiesta Nuts
Savory Ham Supper
Quick Cheese Loaf
Lettuce Wedges *with*
Sour Cream-Vegetable Dressing
Crème de Cacao Pie
Beverage

Preparation tip: *Save time by preparing the nuts, salad dressing, and pie in advance. Bake ham dish and bread together, but take the bread out when it's done. The ham supper finishes baking alone.*

Fiesta Nuts

Use as an appetizer or a TV snack —

　¼ **cup cooking oil**
1½ **teaspoons chili powder**
　1 **teaspoon Worcestershire sauce**
　½ **teaspoon cayenne**
　½ **teaspoon garlic salt**
　2 **cups unroasted cashews**
　2 **cups unroasted pecans**

In a small mixing bowl combine oil, chili powder, Worcestershire sauce, cayenne, and garlic salt. Add cashews; toss to coat. Spread in an 11x7½x1½-inch baking pan. Bake at 300° for 15 minutes. Add pecans, stirring to coat. Continue baking 1 hour, stirring the mixture frequently. Sprinkle with additional salt, if desired. Makes 4 cups.

Savory Ham Supper

Fruit and vegetable team up with meat in this color-ful main dish—

> 1 2-pound fully cooked ham slice, cut
>   1 inch thick
> 2 medium acorn squash
> 1 8-ounce can whole cranberry sauce
> ⅓ cup packed brown sugar
> ¼ cup orange juice
> ½ teaspoon ground cinnamon
>   Dash ground cloves
>
>   • • •
>
> 3 baking apples
> ¼ cup packed brown sugar
> 2 tablespoons butter *or* margarine
> 2 tablespoons cold water
> 2 tablespoons cornstarch

Slash fat edge of ham. Place ham slice on rack in large, shallow baking pan. Cut each acorn squash into fourths; remove seeds. Place squash, skin side up, in baking pan around ham. Bake at 350° for 30 minutes. Meanwhile, in saucepan combine cranberry sauce, ⅓ cup brown sugar, orange juice, cinnamon, and cloves. Bring to boiling; reduce heat and simmer, uncovered, for 5 minutes.

Core and halve apples; place, skin side down, around ham. Spoon cranberry glaze over ham and apples. Turn squash pieces skin side down; sprinkle with salt and the ¼ cup brown sugar. Dot with butter or margarine. Continue baking for 40 minutes. Remove ham, squash, and apples to serving platter. Measure pan juices and add water to make 2 cups. Pour into saucepan. Stir the 2 tablespoons cold water into the cornstarch. Add to pan juices. Cook and stir till thickened and bubbly. Pass with ham dinner. Serves 6.

Sour Cream-Vegetable Dressing

Prepare this easy-to-make dressing ahead—

Combine ½ cup finely chopped cucumber, 2 tablespoons finely chopped green pepper, 2 tablespoons sliced radish, and 2 table-spoons sliced green onion. Stir in 1 cup dairy sour cream, 1 teaspoon lemon juice, ½ tea-spoon salt, and dash pepper; chill thoroughly. Serve dressing over wedges of lettuce. Serves 6.

Quick Cheese Loaf

> 1 beaten egg
> 1 cup milk
> 1 tablespoon instant minced onion
>   Few drops bottled hot pepper sauce
> 3 cups packaged biscuit mix
> ¾ cup grated Cheddar cheese
>   (3 ounces)
>   Butter *or* margarine

In bowl combine egg, milk, onion, and hot pepper sauce. Let stand 5 minutes. Meanwhile, stir together biscuit mix and cheese. Stir in milk mixture just to moisten. Turn into 3 greased 6x3x2-inch loaf pans. Bake at 350° till done, 25 to 30 minutes. Let stand in pans 5 minutes. Turn out on wire rack to cool. Serve with butter. Makes 3 small loaves.

Crème de Cacao Pie

> 1 envelope unflavored gelatin
> 2 egg yolks
> ½ cup sugar
> 2 1-ounce squares unsweetened
>   chocolate
> 1 cup milk
> 2 tablespoons crème de cacao
> 2 egg whites
> ½ cup sugar
> 1 4½-ounce container frozen whipped
>   dessert topping, thawed
> 1 *baked* 9-inch pastry shell, cooled

Soften gelatin in ¼ cup water. Beat egg yolks till thick and lemon-colored. Gradually beat in the ½ cup sugar; add dash salt. In sauce-pan combine chocolate and ½ *cup* of the milk; stir over low heat till the chocolate is melted. Stir in softened gelatin till dissolved. Immediately beat chocolate mixture into egg yolk mixture. Add the remaining ½ cup milk and crème de cacao, beating till well blended. Chill till mixture is partially set.

Beat egg whites to soft peaks. Gradually add ½ cup sugar; beat to stiff peaks. Fold into chocolate mixture. Fold in *1 cup* of the whipped topping. Pile into cooled pastry shell. Chill till firm, 4 to 6 hours. Serve garnished with remaining topping.

HOLIDAY DINNER

Apricot-Glazed Turkey
Vegetable-Rice Casserole
Broccoli Spears
Hot Rolls   Butter
Rosé Fruit Mold
Poached Ruby Pears
Beverage

Preparation tip: *Make the salad in advance and chill well. Prepare and roast the turkey according to the Poultry roasting chart. While the turkey is roasting, assemble the casserole and dessert. Stagger the cooking times so that everything will be ready at the same time.*

Apricot-Glazed Turkey

Glaze gives this turkey a rich, golden color—

    1 8- to 10-pound ready-to-cook turkey
    Salt
    Pepper
    Melted butter *or* margarine
        • • •
    ¼ cup apricot preserves
    ¼ cup honey
    1 tablespoon bottled steak sauce
    1 tablespoon lemon juice
    2 teaspoons cornstarch

Sprinkle neck and body cavities of the turkey with salt and pepper. Fasten neck skin to back of bird; twist wing tips till they rest flat against back of bird. Tuck legs under band of skin, or tie legs together and fasten to tail. Place bird on rack in pan, brush skin with butter, cover with foil tent, and roast according to the chart at 325° for 3½ hours.

Meanwhile, in saucepan combine apricot preserves, honey, steak sauce, lemon juice, and cornstarch. Cook and stir till mixture is slightly thickened and bubbly. Uncover bird; brush with sauce. Following the test for doneness given in the Poultry roasting chart, continue roasting till turkey is done, about 30 minutes longer. Makes 8 servings.

Vegetable-Rice Casserole

Assemble this casserole early in the day, refrigerate, then bake alongside the turkey—

    ⅔ cup long grain rice
    ½ cup chopped onion
    ¼ cup butter *or* margarine
    2 tablespoons all-purpose flour
    1 16-ounce can tomatoes, cut up
    2 12-ounce cans whole kernel corn
        with sweet peppers, drained
    1 teaspoon salt
    ¼ teaspoon bottled hot pepper sauce
    2 slices sharp American cheese
        (2 ounces)

Cook rice according to package directions; set aside. In saucepan cook onion in butter or margarine till tender but not brown. Blend in all-purpose flour. Stir in undrained tomatoes. Cook and stir till mixture thickens and bubbles. Stir in cooked rice, drained corn with peppers, salt, and hot pepper sauce. Turn mixture into ungreased 2-quart casserole. Bake at 325° till heated through, 30 to 35 minutes. Cut each cheese slice into 4 triangles; arrange on top of casserole. Bake 10 minutes longer to melt cheese. Makes 8 servings.

Poached Ruby Pears

A delectable, clear red color makes this the perfect dessert for a holiday dinner—

    2 cups cranberry juice cocktail
    1 3-ounce package strawberry-flavored
        gelatin
        • • •
    8 ripe medium pears (3 pounds),
        peeled and cored
    8 inches stick cinnamon
    8 whole cloves

In saucepan heat cranberry juice cocktail to boiling; add gelatin, stirring to dissolve. Pour mixture into 3-quart baking dish. Add peeled pears, cinnamon, and cloves. Bake, covered, at 325° till pears are tender, 45 to 50 minutes. Turn pears occasionally in syrup. Remove pears from oven; cool slightly, turning frequently in the syrup. Remove spices. Serve warm or cool. Makes 8 servings.

Rosé Fruit Mold

⅓ cup sugar
2 envelopes unflavored gelatin
1 16-ounce can grapefruit sections
1 cup rosé wine
2 tablespoons lemon juice
3 drops red food coloring (optional)
1 cup seedless green grapes, halved
Celery Seed Dressing

In saucepan mix together sugar, gelatin, and ¼ teaspoon salt. Stir in 1½ cups water. Stir over low heat till gelatin dissolves. Drain grapefruit sections; reserve ½ cup syrup. Stir syrup into gelatin; add wine, lemon juice, and food coloring. Chill till partially set. Fold in grapefruit sections and grapes. Turn into 5-cup ring mold. Chill till firm. Unmold on serving plate lined with lettuce, if desired. Serve with Celery Seed Dressing. Makes 8 servings.

Celery Seed Dressing: In small bowl combine ½ cup sugar, ⅓ cup lemon juice, 1 teaspoon celery seed, 1 teaspoon dry mustard, 1 teaspoon paprika, and ½ teaspoon salt. Slowly add ¾ cup salad oil, beating with electric mixer or rotary beater till mixture is thickened. Makes 1⅓ cups dressing.

Poultry roasting chart

General Roasting: Stuff, if desired. Skewer neck skin to back. Tuck legs under band of skin or tie to tail. Place, breast side up, on rack in shallow roasting pan. Rub skin with cooking oil. If meat thermometer is used, insert in center of inside thigh muscle without touching bone. Roast, uncovered, following chart. When bird is ⅔ done, cut skin or string between legs. Roast till done. *Test for Doneness:* The thickest part of the drumstick should feel very soft when pressed between fingers protected with paper toweling. The drumstick should move up and down and twist easily in socket. Meat thermometer should register 185°. *Before Carving:* Let stand 15 minutes to firm up.

Poultry	Ready-to-Cook Weight	Oven Temp.	Guide to Roasting Time	Special Instructions
Turkey	6 - 8 lbs.	325°	3½-4 hrs.	Cover loosely with foil. Press lightly at end of drumsticks and neck, leaving air space between bird and foil. Last 45 minutes, cut band of skin or string between legs. Roast, uncovered, till done.
	8 -12 lbs.	325°	4-4½ hrs.	
	12 -16 lbs.	325°	4½-5½ hrs.	
	16 -20 lbs.	325°	5½-6½ hrs.	
	20 -24 lbs.	325°	6½-7½ hrs.	
Foil-wrapped Turkey	7 - 9 lbs.	450°	2¼-2½ hrs.	Place skewered turkey, breast up, in center of greased, wide, heavy foil. Bring ends of foil up over breast; overlap fold and press up against ends of turkey. Place bird in shallow pan (no rack). Open foil last 20 minutes to brown turkey.
	10 -13 lbs.	450°	2¾-3 hrs.	
	14 -17 lbs.	450°	3-3¼ hrs.	
	18 -21 lbs.	450°	3¼-3½ hrs.	
	22 -24 lbs.	450°	3¼-3¾ hrs.	
Chicken	1½ - 2 lbs.	400°	1-1¼ hrs.	Brush dry areas of skin occasionally with pan drippings. Cover the chicken loosely with foil.
	2½ - 3 lbs.	375°	1¼-1½ hrs.	
	3½ - 4 lbs.	375°	1¾-2 hrs.	
	4½ - 5 lbs.	375°	2¼-2½ hrs.	
Cornish Game Hen	1 -1½ lbs.	375°	1½ hrs.	Roast, loosely covered, for ½ hour, then roast, uncovered, till done, about 1 hour. If desired, baste occasionally with butter the last hour.

Dinners from the freezer

Put your freezer to good use—stock up on foods that are in season and freeze complete meals ahead of serving. Keep a list of menu foods and label them so that you can decide what to serve for dinner at a glance.

ORIENTAL DINNER

Hong Kong Chicken Casserole
Hard Rolls   Butter
Frozen Fruit Salad
Date-Pear Bread Pudding   Cream
Beverage

Preparation tip: *Assemble, then freeze the casserole, salad, and dessert. Start baking the casserole and dessert at same time. After 1 hour, stir casserole and uncover dessert.*

Date-Pear Bread Pudding

```
 5 pears, peeled, cored, and sliced
     (about 5 cups)
 2 tablespoons lemon juice
 ½ cup butter or margarine, melted
 ⅓ cup packed brown sugar
 ½ teaspoon ground allspice
 ¼ teaspoon ground cinnamon
 4 cups fresh bread cubes (5 slices)
 ½ cup chopped pitted dates
 ¼ cup chopped walnuts
   Light cream
```

Mix pears with lemon juice. Combine butter, brown sugar, and spices. Add bread; stir to coat. Spread half the bread mixture in buttered 8x1½-inch round freezer-to-oven baking dish. Top with pears, dates, and nuts. Top with remaining bread mixture. Cover tightly, seal, label, and freeze. To serve, bake frozen dessert, covered, at 400° for 1 hour. Uncover; bake till pears are tender, 5 to 10 minutes longer. Serve warm with cream. Serves 6.

Hong Kong Chicken Casserole

Crisp Chinese vegetables and brightly colored carrots accent this chicken-rice medley—

```
 ⅔ cup long grain rice
 1⅓ cups water
 ½ cup chopped onion
 2 tablespoons cooking oil
 1 10¾-ounce can condensed cream
     of chicken soup
 ¼ cup soy sauce
 1 teaspoon sugar
 3 cups cubed cooked chicken or turkey
 2 cups cubed zucchini
 1 16-ounce can fancy mixed Chinese
     vegetables, drained
 1 cup thinly sliced carrots, cooked
 ½ teaspoon ground ginger
 ½ teaspoon dry mustard
   Soy sauce
```

Cook rice in the 1⅓ cups unsalted water according to package directions; drain rice. In large saucepan cook onion in oil till crisp-tender. Add condensed soup, ¼ cup soy sauce, and sugar. Bring mixture to boiling. Stir in the chicken, zucchini, cooked rice, Chinese vegetables, carrots, ginger, and dry mustard. Cool quickly. Turn mixture into a 2-quart freezer-to-oven baking dish. Cover tightly, seal, label, and freeze. To serve, bake frozen casserole, covered, at 400° for 1 hour. Uncover; stir casserole and bake 30 minutes longer. Pass additional soy sauce. Makes 6 servings.

Savor the flavor of soy sauce mingled with rice and chicken in *Hong Kong Chicken Casserole.* A warm finale to this meal is the *Date-Pear Bread Pudding* served fresh from the oven and drizzled with light cream.

Preparation tip: *Freeze the foods as directed. When you're ready to use this meal, bake the main dish 45 minutes. Then, add the cabbage bundles when you stir the water into the pie; continue baking. Prepare the biscuits, drop on the bubbling hot pie, and finish baking. Bake the dessert just before serving.*

Carrot-Stuffed Cabbage Bundles

     6 medium carrots, cut in thin 3-inch
        strips (3 cups)
    12 large cabbage leaves
           • • •
     2 tablespoons chopped green pepper
     2 tablespoons chopped onion
     2 tablespoons butter *or* margarine
     1 tablespoon lemon juice
     ½ teaspoon dried basil, crushed

Add carrots to small amount of boiling salted water; return to boiling. Cover; reduce heat and cook 6 to 8 minutes. Drain; set aside. Immerse cabbage leaves in boiling salted water just until limp, 2 to 3 minutes; drain.

Combine carrots, green pepper, onion, butter, lemon juice, and crushed basil. Form six stacks of cabbage leaves by placing two cabbage leaves together. Spoon ⅓ cup of the carrot mixture in the center of each cabbage leaf stack; fold in sides and ends over filling. Place cabbage bundles, seam side down, in a 10x6x2-inch freezer-to-oven baking dish. Cover tightly, seal, label, and freeze.

To serve, bake the frozen casserole, covered, at 400° till heated through, about 1 hour. Makes 4 to 6 servings.

Beef-Burgundy Pie

    ¼ cup all-purpose flour
    ½ teaspoon salt
    ¼ teaspoon pepper
     1 pound beef round steak, cut in
        1-inch cubes
     2 tablespoons cooking oil
     1 10½-ounce can condensed beef broth
     1 cup Burgundy
    ¾ cup water
     1 clove garlic, minced
    ¼ teaspoon dried dillweed
    ¼ teaspoon dried marjoram, crushed
     1 9-ounce package frozen artichoke
        hearts
  1½ cups sliced fresh mushrooms
        Drop Biscuits

Mix 2 *tablespoons* flour, salt, and pepper; toss with meat to coat. In 3-quart saucepan brown *half* the meat at a time in hot oil. Spoon off excess fat. Add broth, Burgundy, ½ *cup* water, garlic, dillweed, and marjoram. Cover. Simmer 50 minutes; stir often. Add artichokes and mushrooms; return to boiling. Cover; simmer 10 minutes. Mix remaining flour and water. Stir into beef mixture. Cook and stir till thickened. Cool quickly. Turn into 1½-quart freezer-to-oven casserole. Cover tightly, seal, label, and freeze. To serve, bake frozen casserole, covered, at 400° for 45 minutes; stir in ¾ cup *hot* water. Cover; bake till heated through, about 45 minutes more. Uncover; top with Drop Biscuits. Bake till biscuits brown, 12 to 15 minutes. Makes 4 to 6 servings.

Drop Biscuits: Prepare 1 cup packaged biscuit mix, following package directions for drop biscuits. Drop 6 biscuits atop casserole.

Garbanzo Deluxe

Drain one 15-ounce can garbanzo beans; combine with 2 chopped hard-cooked eggs, ½ cup mayonnaise, ½ cup chopped celery, ¼ cup sliced radishes, 2 tablespoons chopped green pepper, 2 tablespoons chili sauce, 1 tablespoon finely snipped chives, 1 teaspoon paprika, and ½ teaspoon salt. Chill several hours. Before serving, add 2 cups torn lettuce; toss lightly to coat. Makes 6 servings.

Waldorf Molded Salad

1¾ **cups apple juice** *or* **cider**
1 **3-ounce package lemon-flavored gelatin**
 Dash salt
¼ **cup dairy sour cream**
¼ **cup mayonnaise** *or* **salad dressing**
1 **cup diced unpeeled apples**
¼ **cup chopped celery**
¼ **cup chopped walnuts**
 Lettuce

In medium saucepan bring *1 cup* cider to boiling. Add gelatin and dash salt; stir to dissolve. Remove from heat. Add remaining cider. Cool slightly. Combine sour cream and mayonnaise; beat into gelatin. Chill till partially set. Fold in apples, celery, and walnuts. Turn into 6 individual molds. Chill till firm. Unmold onto lettuce-lined plates. Makes 6 servings.

Alaska à l'Orange

Line 1-quart bowl with waxed paper; leave 2-inch overhang. Press 1 quart orange sherbet into bowl; fold paper over sherbet. Freeze firm. Prepare 1 package 1-layer-size yellow cake mix, following package directions. Bake in an 8x1½-inch round baking pan. Cool 10 minutes. Remove to rack underlined with waxed paper. Drizzle ¼ cup orange liqueur over warm cake. Cool. Place on baking sheet.

Beat 3 egg whites with ½ teaspoon vanilla and ¼ teaspoon cream of tartar to soft peaks. Gradually add 6 tablespoons sugar; beat till stiff peaks form. Unmold sherbet onto cake, removing paper. Spread egg white mixture over sherbet and cake. Freeze. Cover with foil; freeze firm. To serve, uncover and place on wooden board; bake at 500° till golden. Place on platter. Garnish with 1 tablespoon grated orange peel. Makes 6 servings.

Make spectacular *Beef-Burgundy Pie* the main dish of a meal that has all been made ahead and frozen. When you serve this ragout, you won't need to coax your family to the table.

You'd be surprised at what a few seasonings do for *Fish Fillets Olé*—the chili powder makes this dish fiery, while a tomato sauce mixture adds extra flavor to the fish. And try a few slices of lemon and a sprig or two of watercress for a colorful, last-minute garnish.

FISH DAY FAVORITE

Fish Fillets Olé
Sweet Pickles
Poppy Seed Rolls   Butter
Sour Cream Coleslaw *or*
Strawberry Yogurt Medley
Apple-Nutty Crisp   Ice Cream
Beverage

Preparation tip: *Make and chill coleslaw or fruit medley. Bake the frozen casserole and dessert together. Remove the dessert after 50 minutes and let cool slightly.*

Strawberry Yogurt Medley

    2 medium oranges, peeled
    2 medium bananas
    2 cups fresh strawberries, halved
    ½ cup strawberry yogurt
    1 4-ounce container whipped cream
        cheese
    2 tablespoons sugar
      Lettuce

Section oranges, reserving the juice. Slice bananas and dip in reserved orange juice. In bowl combine orange sections, bananas, and strawberries; chill. Stir yogurt into cream cheese; stir in sugar. Arrange fruit in compote; spoon yogurt mixture over or stir topping into fruit. Serve in lettuce cups. Serves 4 to 6.

Fish Fillets Olé

2 cups cooked rice
1 10-ounce package frozen Mexican-
    style vegetables, partially thawed
¼ teaspoon chili powder
¼ teaspoon ground cumin
    Dash garlic salt
¼ cup chopped onion
1 tablespoon butter *or* margarine
1 15-ounce can tomato sauce
¾ cup water
1 14-ounce package frozen loose-pack
    haddock *or* other fish fillets

Combine cooked rice, partially thawed vegetables, chili powder, cumin, and garlic salt. Spoon into 11x7½x1½-inch freezer-to-oven baking dish. In saucepan cook onion in butter till tender but not brown. Stir in tomato sauce and water. Top the vegetable-rice mixture with frozen fish fillets. Sprinkle with salt. Pour tomato mixture over fish.

Cover tightly, seal, label, and freeze. To serve, bake frozen casserole, covered, at 400° till fish flakes easily when tested with a fork, about 1½ hours. Before serving, trim with lemon slices and sprigs of watercress, if desired. Makes 4 servings.

Sour Cream Coleslaw

The tang of sour cream is a palate-pleaser in its use as an ingredient for coleslaw dressing—

½ cup dairy sour cream
1½ teaspoons vinegar
1 teaspoon sugar
½ teaspoon salt
    Dash pepper
¼ cup shredded carrot
1 tablespoon thinly sliced radish
1 tablespoon finely chopped green
    pepper
1 tablespoon finely chopped green
    onion
3 cups shredded cabbage

In a bowl combine the sour cream, vinegar, sugar, salt, and pepper. Fold in carrot, radish, green pepper, and onion. Pour over cabbage; mix lightly. Makes 4 servings.

Apple-Nutty Crisp

A peanut butter-flavored apple crisp served with scoops of vanilla ice cream—

3 cups sliced peeled tart apples
    Ascorbic acid color keeper
        • • •
½ cup sugar
½ cup all-purpose flour
⅛ teaspoon ground ginger
3 tablespoons butter *or* margarine
3 tablespoons chunk-style peanut
    butter
        • • •
    Vanilla ice cream

Treat apples with ascorbic acid color keeper according to directions on the label. Place apples in an 8-inch freezer-to-oven pie plate. Stir together the sugar, flour, and ginger till thoroughly combined; cut in the butter and peanut butter till the mixture is crumbly. Sprinkle topping over apples. Cover tightly, seal, label, and freeze.

To serve, bake frozen dessert, covered, at 400° for 30 minutes. Uncover and continue baking till apples are tender and topping is crisp, about 20 minutes. Serve warm with vanilla ice cream. Makes 4 servings.

Freezing know-how

- To ensure high quality in your frozen food products, it is good practice to keep an up-to-date inventory of the freezer stockpile.
- Baking dishes used for freezing casseroles or other oven meal recipes should be of the freezer-to-oven type. Ceramic glass cookware is one type that will successfully go from the freezer to a hot oven then directly to the dinner table.
- Prepare double batches of a favorite dish and freeze one for future use. To free a casserole dish for reuse, line it with foil, fill dish, cover with foil, and freeze food till solid. The food is easily removable and it retains the shape of its baking container, which is used later during baking.

The time-controlled oven

Programmed oven meals are ideal for the homemaker who wants to put the evening meal in the oven at noon. These time-controlled menus delay the start of cooking for a relatively short period of time.

ITALIAN-STYLE SUPPER

Italian Braciole
Spaghetti   Parmesan Cheese
Savory Green Beans
Tomato and Cucumber Salad
Elegant Fruit Combo   Ice Cream
Beverage

Preparation tip: *Check your oven's "use and care" booklet to be sure you know how to operate the programming clock properly. Make the meat rolls ahead of time and freeze. When ready to start meal, make the beans and dessert and place all three food dishes in the time-controlled oven at the same time.*

Elegant Fruit Combo

Ice cream adds a cooling touch—

    1 16-ounce can peach halves
    1 cup fresh cranberries
    ¼ cup sugar
    1 large banana, sliced
    1 pint vanilla ice cream

Drain peaches and reserve the syrup. Place peach halves in a bowl, cover tightly, and set aside. In 1-quart casserole combine the reserved peach syrup, cranberries, and sugar. Cover casserole and place in oven. Following directions for your oven, set programming clock to bake at 350° for 1¼ hours.

To serve, remove from oven and stir in reserved peach halves and banana slices. Top each serving with a scoop of vanilla ice cream. Makes 6 servings.

Italian Braciole

Cut 2 pounds ¼-inch-thick beef round steak into 6 rectangular pieces; pound flat. Season with salt and pepper. Spread meat with ½ cup chopped onion to within ½ inch of edge. Roll up jelly-roll fashion; secure with wooden picks. Place, seam side down, in 10x6x2-inch baking dish. Mix ¼ cup chili sauce; ¼ cup condensed beef broth; one 3-ounce can sliced mushrooms, drained; 2 tablespoons chopped green pepper; 2 tablespoons sliced pimiento-stuffed green olives; 1 teaspoon sugar; 1 teaspoon Worcestershire sauce; ¼ teaspoon dried oregano, crushed; ⅛ teaspoon garlic powder; and ⅛ teaspoon pepper. Pour over meat rolls. Cover tightly, seal, label, and freeze.

To bake, place frozen meat rolls in oven *no more than 4 hours before baking begins.* Set programming clock to bake at 350° for 1¼ hours. (Add extra cooking time if meal waits less than the 4 hours.) To serve, remove rolls. Add water to pan juices to make 1½ cups. Blend ½ cup cold water into 3 tablespoons all-purpose flour. Add to pan juices. Cook and stir till thickened. Pass gravy. Serves 6.

Savory Green Beans

In 1-quart casserole mix two 9-ounce packages frozen cut green beans; ¼ cup chopped onion; ¼ cup melted butter; ¾ teaspoon salt; and ½ teaspoon dried savory, crushed. Cover; put in oven. Set programming clock to bake at 350° for 1¼ hours. Stir. Serves 6.

When you can't be home all day, bake *Italian Braciole, Savory Green Beans,* and *Elegant Fruit Compote* in a time-controlled oven. ▶

SUNDAY DINNER

Oven-Crisped Chicken
Baked Potatoes
Zippy Baked Asparagus
Apricot Soufflé Salad
Mince-Apple Pie *with*
Ice Cream
Beverage

Preparation tip: *Scrub, dry, and prick medium baking potatoes. Wrap in foil and place in the oven with the frozen chicken, asparagus, and pie. Following instructions for your oven's programming clock, set the clock to begin baking 1½ hours before serving time. Remove the pie along with the potatoes, chicken, and asparagus and let pie cool while you eat the main course.*

Oven-Crisped Chicken

Onion salad dressing mix adds the extra zing to this easy-to-make chicken dish —

> ½ **cup finely crushed rich round crackers (12 crackers)**
> 1 **envelope onion salad dressing mix (about 2 tablespoons)**
> ½ **teaspoon paprika**
>   • • •
> 1 **2½- to 3-pound ready-to-cook broiler-fryer chicken, cut up**
> ¼ **cup butter** *or* **margarine, melted**
> 2 **tablespoons sesame seed**

Combine cracker crumbs, salad dressing mix, and paprika. Dip the chicken pieces in the melted butter or margarine, then coat lightly with the cracker mixture. Place chicken in a 13x9x2-inch baking pan. Drizzle with the remaining butter. Sprinkle sesame seed over chicken pieces. Cover pan tightly, seal, label, and freeze.

To bake, uncover and place frozen chicken in oven *no more than 4 hours before baking begins.* Set programming clock to bake at 350° for 1½ hours. Makes 4 servings.

Zippy Baked Asparagus

> 1 **10½-ounce can condensed cream of celery soup**
> 1 **tablespoon all-purpose flour**
> 1 **teaspoon prepared horseradish**
> 1 **teaspoon Worcestershire sauce**
> 1 **teaspoon prepared mustard**
> 2 **10-ounce packages frozen cut asparagus, broken apart**

In bowl combine soup, flour, horseradish, Worcestershire, and mustard. Stir in asparagus. Turn into 1-quart freezer-to-oven casserole. Cover tightly, seal, label, and freeze. To bake, set programming clock to bake at 350° till asparagus is tender, about 1½ hours. Serve in individual dishes. Serves 4.

Apricot Soufflé Salad

Dissolve one 3-ounce package orange-flavored gelatin in 1 cup boiling water; add ½ cup cold water and 2 tablespoons lemon juice. Gradually stir into ½ cup mayonnaise. Chill till partially set. Meanwhile, drain one 16-ounce can peeled whole apricots; slice apricots and arrange in 3-cup mold. Whip partially set gelatin till fluffy. Fold in ¼ cup chopped celery; spoon into mold. Chill till firm. Serves 4 to 6.

Mince-Apple Pie

>   **Pastry for 2-crust 9-inch pie**
> 1 **18-ounce jar prepared mincemeat**
> ½ **cup chopped walnuts**
> 2 **tablespoons brandy**
> 1 **tablespoon all-purpose flour**
> 3 **tart medium apples, peeled, cored, and sliced (3 cups)**
>   **Vanilla ice cream**

Line a 9-inch pie plate with pastry. Combine mincemeat, walnuts, brandy, and flour. Mix with apples. Turn into pastry shell. Cover with top crust; cut slits for escape of steam. Cover tightly, seal, label, and freeze. To bake, uncover pie and place in oven. Set programming clock to bake at 350° for 1½ hours. Serve with ice cream. Makes 6 to 8 servings.

SUPPER AFTER THE GAME

Sausage-Lamb Cassoulet
Relishes
Fruited Cottage Cheese Ring
French Bread   Butter
Butterscotch-Rice Pudding
Beverage

Preparation tip: *For thorough chilling, make the relishes and salad early in the day or the night before. Prepare the pudding and place it in the oven with the cassoulet. Following directions for your oven, set the programming clock to start baking 1½ hours before serving time. Don't let the cassoulet sit in the oven more than 4 hours before cooking begins.*

Sausage-Lamb Cassoulet

A superior blend of flavors makes this an excellent version of the French classic —

> 3 15-ounce cans great northern beans, drained
> 1 cup dry white wine
> 1 8-ounce can tomato sauce
> ¾ cup chopped onion
> 1 tablespoon snipped parsley
> 2 bay leaves
> 1 clove garlic, minced
> ½ teaspoon dried thyme, crushed
> 8 ounces boneless lamb, cut in ½-inch cubes
> 2 tablespoons cooking oil
> 8 ounces Polish sausage, sliced ½ inch thick (4 sausages)

In a 3-quart casserole combine beans, wine, tomato sauce, onion, parsley, bay leaves, garlic, and thyme. Cook lamb in hot oil till well browned on all sides; drain off excess oil. Add lamb and sliced sausage to bean mixture; stir. *No more than 4 hours before baking begins,* place covered casserole in oven. Set programming clock to bake at 325° for 1½ hours. Remove and discard bay leaves before serving in bowls. Makes 6 to 8 servings.

Fruited Cottage Cheese Ring

> 1 envelope unflavored gelatin
> 2 tablespoons lemon juice
> ¼ teaspoon salt
> 1 cup whipping cream
> 2 cups cream-style cottage cheese
> 3 cups cut-up mixed fresh fruit

Soften gelatin in ¼ cup water. In saucepan combine softened gelatin, the lemon juice, ¼ teaspoon salt, and dash pepper; heat till the gelatin dissolves. Cool to room temperature. Whip cream; combine with cottage cheese and gelatin mixture. Pour into a 5-cup ring mold. Chill till set. Unmold onto serving plate; fill center with the fresh fruit. Serves 6 to 8.

Butterscotch-Rice Pudding

> 2½ cups water
> ¾ cup long grain rice
> ⅓ cup packed brown sugar
> ⅛ teaspoon ground nutmeg
> 1 18-ounce can butterscotch pudding
> Whipped cream *or* whipped topping

In 2-quart casserole combine water, uncooked rice, sugar, nutmeg, and ⅛ teaspoon salt. Cover. Place casserole in oven. Set programming clock to bake at 325° for 1½ hours. Before serving, fold in butterscotch pudding. Top each serving with whipped cream or whipped topping. Makes 6 to 8 servings.

Delay-cooking safety tips

Time-controlled cooking has many advantages for the busy homemaker, but keep these things in mind: these menus are meant to delay the start of cooking no more than 4 hours—postponing the start of cooking longer may result in food spoilage; *unless frozen,* avoid using food dishes that contain milk, eggs, fish, poultry, and pork, and meats that are handled extensively; and allow for thawing when figuring cooking time of frozen foods in a delay-cook oven.

All-Temperature Oven Recipes

Build menus around a particular oven temperature. In a slow oven cook Shrimp and Tuna Bake and Carrot-Cheddar Casserole. Bake Cottage Cheese Buns and Vera Cruz Tomatoes in a moderate oven. Then, turn the oven temperature up to hot for Fresh Pear Dumplings. (See index for page numbers.)

Slow oven dishes

Dishes baked slow and easy (300° to 325° F.) require very little attention. And the meal planning is a cinch because the wide time range provides ample leeway to fix the rest of the meal or free time to relax.

Ham with Apricot-Mustard Glaze

 1 3-pound canned ham
 ¼ cup apricot preserves
 1 tablespoon light corn syrup
 1 tablespoon prepared mustard
 1 tablespoon butter *or* margarine
 2 tablespoons chopped walnuts

Place ham on rack in shallow roasting pan. Roast at 325° for 1 hour. Cut diamond pattern atop ham. Combine preserves, corn syrup, mustard, and butter. Bring mixture to boiling; spread over ham. Sprinkle top with walnuts. Bake till a meat thermometer registers 160°, 30 minutes more. Makes 6 servings.

Corned Pork Loin

Refrigerate 10 days in brine before cooking—

 1 4- to 5-pound boneless pork
  loin roast
 ½ cup salt
 2 tablespoons sugar
 2 quarts water
 2 cloves garlic, minced
 2 tablespoons mixed pickling spices
 2 teaspoons instant minced onion

Place meat in crock or large, deep bowl (not metal). (Cut meat in half to make it fit, if necessary.) Dissolve salt and sugar in the water. Stir in garlic, spices, and onion. Pour over meat. Cover meat with a plate and weight it down to keep meat immersed. Refrigerate 10 days; turn meat occasionally.

 Drain off brine; cover meat with water and soak 1 to 2 hours. Drain; pat dry with paper toweling. Roast, uncovered, in shallow roasting pan at 325° till meat thermometer registers 170°, 2½ to 3 hours. Serves 12 to 15.

Rice-Apricot Stuffed Pork

Be sure the meatman loosens the backbone—

 ½ cup chopped dried apricots
 2¾ cups water
 2 tablespoons sugar
  • • •
 1 cup long grain rice
 ½ cup chopped onion
 ¼ cup snipped parsley
 ¼ cup butter *or* margarine
 2 teaspoons grated lemon peel
 1 teaspoon salt
 ⅛ teaspoon pepper
 1 4- to 4½-pound pork loin roast

Rinse apricots; place in saucepan with water and sugar. Bring to boiling; reduce heat. Cover and simmer 5 minutes. Stir in rice, onion, parsley, butter or margarine, lemon peel, salt, and pepper. Simmer till rice is tender, 25 to 30 minutes; cool.

 Remove backbone from roast. Without cutting ribs apart, make deep slit between each rib bone along fat side of roast. Stuff about 3 tablespoons rice mixture into each slit; pack firmly. Place roast, fat side up, on rack in shallow roasting pan. Roast at 325° for 30 minutes; cover stuffing with foil.

 Continue roasting till meat thermometer registers 170°, 2 to 2½ hours. Place remaining stuffing in 1-quart casserole; salt lightly. Bake last 20 minutes of roasting time. Let roast stand 10 minutes before carving. Makes 8 servings.

Transform the mild flavor of pork into a roast ❯ with character. Pull out the crock and immerse the boneless roast in a spicy brine. The 10 days in the well-seasoned homemade brine will give the *Corned Pork Loin* a full-bodied flavor.

Ham and Cheese Bake

Remove crusts from 8 slices white bread. Place *4 slices* of the trimmed bread in a single layer in greased 8x8x2-inch baking dish. Mix 2 cups ground fully cooked ham and 2 tablespoons prepared mustard. Spread ham mixture over bread. Sprinkle 2 cups shredded American cheese (8 ounces) atop.

Cut remaining bread on the diagonal and place in two rows over cheese. (Bases should overlap at points of preceding 'triangles'.) Combine 3 beaten eggs, 2 cups milk, and dash pepper. Pour over bread mixture. Chill 1 hour. Bake at 325° for 55 to 60 minutes. Serves 6.

Ham Royale

 1 cup packed brown sugar
 ¾ cup orange juice
 ½ cup dry sherry
 2 tablespoons prepared mustard
   Dash ground cloves
 1 5-pound canned ham
 2 tablespoons cornstarch

Combine first five ingredients. Place ham in shallow dish; prick with a fork. Pour sherry mixture over ham. Marinate in refrigerator several hours; turn occasionally. Remove ham and drain, reserving marinade. Place ham on rack in shallow roasting pan. Bake at 325° till meat thermometer registers 140°, about 1½ hours. Baste often with marinade. Remove ham to warm platter; reserve pan juices. Blend 2 tablespoons cold water into cornstarch; stir into pan juices. Cook and stir till mixture bubbles. Pass sauce with ham. Serves 15.

Is preheating necessary?

Not always. Although all the recipes in this book were tested in preheated ovens for consistency, many of the long-cooking recipes don't need a preheated oven. However, be sure to preheat the oven when baking leavened products, such as cakes, cookies, breads, and delicate dishes such as soufflés.

Leg of Lamb Italian

 ⅓ cup lemon juice
 ¼ cup cooking oil
 1 tablespoon dried oregano, crushed
 2 teaspoons chopped anchovies
 1 teaspoon dry mustard
 1 teaspoon salt
 ½ teaspoon garlic powder
      • • •
 1 5- to 6-pound whole lamb leg
 ¼ cup cold water
 ¼ cup all-purpose flour

In a bowl combine lemon juice, oil, oregano, anchovies, mustard, salt, and garlic powder. Place lamb in plastic bag; set in deep bowl. Pour lemon juice mixture in bag; close tightly. Marinate in refrigerator overnight, pressing bag occasionally to distribute marinade. Drain meat, reserving marinade; place meat, fat side up, on rack in shallow roasting pan. Roast at 325° till meat thermometer registers 175° to 180°, 3 to 3½ hours, basting occasionally with marinade. Remove to warm platter.

Skim the fat from meat juices; pour brown bits and juices into large measuring cup. Add enough remaining marinade to measure 2¼ cups liquid. Blend cold water into flour; stir into marinade mixture in saucepan. Cook and stir till thickened and bubbly. Serve with roast. Makes 8 to 10 servings.

Savory Stuffed Rib Roast

 4 ounces thinly sliced ham, chopped
   (1 cup)
 3 slices bacon, snipped
 ¼ cup chopped onion
 2 tablespoons chopped pimiento-stuffed
   green olives
 1 clove garlic, minced
 1 beaten egg
 1 4- to 5-pound boneless beef rib
   roast (rolled and tied)

In a bowl combine ham, bacon, onion, olives, garlic, and egg. Unroll roast; spread ham mixture over meat. Reroll and tie roast securely; place on rack in shallow roasting pan. Roast at 325° till done, 2½ to 3 hours. Serves 12 to 14.

Rump Roast Supreme

    1 4- to 6-pound boneless beef round
        rump roast (rolled and tied)
    2 tablespoons shortening
    1 cup dry red wine
    1 cup beef broth
    ½ cup chopped onion
    1 bay leaf
    1 clove garlic, crushed
    1 teaspoon salt
    ¼ teaspoon ground thyme
    ¼ teaspoon pepper
        Water
    ¼ cup all-purpose flour

In Dutch oven brown the meat slowly on all sides in hot shortening. Add *half* of the dry red wine, the beef broth, onion, bay leaf, garlic, salt, thyme, and pepper. Cover; place in a 325° oven till meat is tender, 2½ to 3 hours. Remove strings; discard. Transfer to serving platter; keep warm. Discard bay leaf. Skim off excess fat; add water to juices to make 2 cups. Blend remaining dry red wine into flour. Return juices to pan; stir flour mixture into juices. Cook, stirring constantly, till thickened and bubbly. Pass with meat. Serves 8 to 10.

Peach-Glazed Corned Beef

    1 3-pound boneless corned beef brisket
    4 small apples, halved lengthwise
    ⅓ cup peach preserves
    ¼ teaspoon ground ginger

Rinse corned beef in cold water to remove the pickling juices. Place the roast, fat side up, on a rack in a shallow roasting pan. Pour in 2 cups water; cover pan with foil. Place in a 325° oven for 2 hours. Remove the foil and drain liquid from pan; discard.

Core apples; arrange apple halves, skin side up, around corned beef. Add ½ cup fresh water. Return to oven and continue cooking, uncovered, 30 minutes longer. Combine the peach preserves and ground ginger. Turn apple halves skin side down. Spoon peach glaze over apple halves and corned beef; continue cooking till glaze is hot, about 15 minutes longer. Makes 6 to 8 servings.

Cheesy Round Steak

    2 tablespoons all-purpose
        flour
    ¼ teaspoon salt
    1 pound beef round steak, cut
        ½ inch thick
        • • •
    2 tablespoons cooking oil
    ½ cup water
    1 teaspoon instant minced onion
    2 slices American cheese, halved

Combine flour and salt; coat steak with mixture. Pound meat to ¼-inch thickness. Cut into 4 serving-size pieces. In oven-going skillet brown the meat slowly in hot oil. Add water and onion. Cover; place in a 325° oven till meat is tender, about 1 hour, adding more water if necessary. Place a *half slice* of cheese atop each piece of meat; cover and heat till cheese melts. Makes 4 servings.

Sour Creamed Pot Roast

    2 slices bacon
    1 3- to 4-pound beef chuck pot roast
    ¾ cup chopped onion
    ¾ cup water
    1 teaspoon salt
    ½ teaspoon ground cumin
    ⅛ teaspoon pepper
        • • •
    2 tablespoons all-purpose flour
    ½ cup dairy sour cream

Cook bacon till crisp; drain, reserving drippings. Crumble bacon and set aside. In Dutch oven brown the chuck roast on both sides in bacon drippings. Add chopped onion, water, salt, ground cumin, and pepper. Cover tightly and place in a 325° oven till meat is tender, 1½ to 2 hours. Remove roast to a warm platter; keep hot. To make gravy, skim excess fat off meat drippings. Blend flour and sour cream. Gradually stir moderate amount of meat drippings into sour cream mixture; return to hot mixture in Dutch oven. Cook and stir till thickened; *do not boil*. Stir in the crumbled bacon. Serve the pot roast with the sour cream gravy. Makes 6 to 8 servings.

Shrimp and Tuna Bake

Seafood medley shown on pages 38 and 39—

    ⅔ cup long grain rice
  1 9-ounce package frozen cut green
      beans
  1 10½-ounce can condensed cream of
      celery soup
    ½ cup milk
  2 tablespoons chopped canned pimiento
    ¼ teaspoon dried thyme, crushed
      Dash cayenne
  1 6½- or 7-ounce can tuna, drained and
      broken into chunks
  1 4½-ounce can shrimp, drained
    ½ of a 3½-ounce can French-fried
      onions (about 1 cup)

Cook rice according to package directions. Cook green beans according to package directions. Drain; set aside. Combine next 5 ingredients; stir till smooth. Stir *half* of sauce mixture into rice; fold in tuna. Turn into a 1½-quart casserole. Spread green beans over rice; top with shrimp. Pour remaining sauce over all. Bake, covered, at 325° till heated through, 25 to 30 minutes. Uncover and sprinkle onions over top; bake till onions are crisp, about 5 minutes longer. Makes 6 servings.

Yam and Sausage Casserole

Slow cooking blends the flavors in this country-style casserole—

In a large skillet cook 1 pound bulk pork sausage with ¾ cup chopped onion and ¼ cup chopped celery till meat is brown and vegetables are tender, about 15 minutes; drain off excess fat. Stir in 1 teaspoon salt; 1 teaspoon lemon juice; ½ teaspoon rubbed sage; ⅛ teaspoon dried thyme, crushed; and ⅛ teaspoon pepper. Set aside.

Peel and shred 3 large uncooked yams *or* sweet potatoes (about 2 pounds); transfer the yams to a large mixing bowl. Stir in cooked sausage and vegetables; mix well. Transfer the mixture to a 2-quart casserole, packing down lightly. Pour ¼ cup water over all. Cover and bake at 325° till yams are very tender, about 1½ hours, stirring the mixture occasionally. Makes 6 servings.

Halibut with Dill Topping

  6 fresh or frozen halibut steaks *or*
      other fish steaks
  3 tablespoons lemon juice
    ½ teaspoon salt
    ¼ teaspoon paprika
      Dash pepper
    ½ cup finely chopped onion
  2 tablespoons butter *or* margarine
    ¼ cup dairy sour cream
  2 tablespoons mayonnaise *or* salad
      dressing
  1 teaspoon dried dillweed

Thaw frozen fish. Arrange fish in a single layer in 13x9x2-inch baking dish. Brush a mixture of the lemon juice, salt, paprika, and dash pepper over both sides of fish. Let stand 30 minutes. Meanwhile, cook onion in butter till tender. Top fish with onion and butter. Bake, uncovered, at 325° till fish flakes easily when tested with fork, 20 to 25 minutes. Combine remaining ingredients. Serve over fish. Serves 6.

Cheese Soufflés à l'Asparagus

In saucepan melt 6 tablespoons butter; blend in ⅓ cup all-purpose flour. Stir in 2 cups milk; cook and stir till thick and bubbly. Add 3 cups shredded sharp American cheese (12 ounces); stir till melted. Remove from heat. Separate 6 eggs. Beat egg yolks till thick and lemon-colored. Gradually stir cheese mixture into yolks. Cool slightly. Beat egg whites with ½ teaspoon cream of tartar till stiff peaks form.

Fold yolk mixture into whites. Spoon into 8 ungreased 1-cup soufflé dishes. Place in baking pan on oven rack. Fill pan with hot water to depth of ½ inch. Bake at 300° till knife inserted off-center comes out clean, 35 to 40 minutes. Serve with Asparagus Sauce. Serves 8.

Asparagus Sauce: In saucepan cook ¼ cup chopped onion in 2 tablespoons butter *or* margarine till tender. Blend in 2 tablespoons all-purpose flour. Add 1½ cups milk and 1 chicken bouillon cube. Cook and stir till thickened and bubbly and bouillon cube is dissolved. Stir in one 10-ounce package frozen cut asparagus, cooked and drained. Heat the asparagus mixture thoroughly.

Don't plan on leftovers with these entrées— you'll savor every bite. Drizzle classic *Cheese Soufflés à l'Asparagus* with velvety sauce and spark *Home-Style Lima Casserole* with a bit of wine. As the perfect partner for either main dish, use a molded fruit salad.

Home-Style Lima Casserole

This hearty dish is made extra good with sausage and tender meatballs in rich gravy—

½ **pound bulk pork sausage**
1 **beaten egg**
½ **cup fine dry bread crumbs**
½ **cup chopped onion**
¼ **cup chopped green pepper**
½ **teaspoon salt**
½ **teaspoon dried marjoram, crushed**
  Dash pepper
1 **pound ground beef**
2 **15-ounce cans dried lima beans**
2 **tablespoons all-purpose flour**
½ **cup water**
⅓ **cup dry white wine**
1 **teaspoon beef-flavored gravy base**
  Dash pepper

In a 10-inch skillet cook sausage till lightly browned. Drain sausage and set aside. Combine egg, bread crumbs, onion, green pepper, salt, marjoram, and dash pepper. Mix in the ground beef. Mix well and shape the mixture into 30 small meatballs. In same skillet brown the meatballs on all sides; remove from heat and set meatballs aside. Drain the canned lima beans, reserving 1 cup of the liquid. Stir the flour into the drippings in skillet. Add the reserved bean liquid, water, wine, gravy base, and dash pepper. Cook and stir till mixture is thickened and bubbly.

Combine sausage, meatballs, beans, and gravy. Spoon into a 2-quart casserole. Bake, covered, at 325° for 40 minutes. Uncover and bake till heated through, 20 to 25 minutes longer. If desired, garnish with green pepper rings and parsley. Makes 6 to 8 servings.

Coq au Vin Blanc

An elegant cream sauce laced with dry white wine makes this dish unforgettable—

¼ **cup all-purpose flour**
1 **teaspoon paprika**
½ **teaspoon salt**
¼ **teaspoon pepper**
1 **2½- to 3-pound ready-to-cook broiler-fryer chicken, cut up**
3 **tablespoons butter *or* margarine**
½ **cup dry white wine**
½ **cup chicken broth**
2 **tablespoons chopped onion**
1 **tablespoon snipped parsley**
¼ **teaspoon dried thyme, crushed**
¼ **teaspoon rubbed sage**

• • •

2 **egg yolks**
¼ **cup light cream**
1 **16-ounce can boiled onions, drained**
1 **3-ounce can sliced mushrooms, drained**
  Salt
  Pepper
  Hot cooked noodles

Combine the flour, paprika, ½ teaspoon salt, and ¼ teaspoon pepper in a paper or plastic bag. Add 2 or 3 pieces of chicken at a time and shake to coat thoroughly. In a skillet melt the butter or margarine over medium heat. Brown the chicken pieces on all sides in the butter. Transfer chicken pieces to a 3-quart casserole. Combine the dry white wine, chicken broth, chopped onion, snipped parsley, thyme, and sage. Pour over chicken in casserole. Bake, covered, at 325° till chicken is tender, about 1 hour. Transfer the chicken pieces to a warm serving platter; keep hot while preparing the sauce.

Pour mixture from casserole into a saucepan. Reduce sauce mixture to 1 cup over high heat, 12 to 15 minutes. Meanwhile, beat the egg yolks and light cream together. Stir a moderate amount of the hot sauce mixture into the egg yolk mixture. Return to hot sauce and stir till combined. Stir in the onions and sliced mushrooms. Season with salt and pepper to taste. Heat sauce just till hot *(do not boil)* and pour over the chicken pieces. Serve with noodles. Makes 6 servings.

Turkey with Meaty Stuffing

Team three kinds of ground meat with chopped spinach for a hearty stuffing—

1 **10-ounce package frozen chopped spinach**
1 **pound bulk pork sausage**
8 **ounces ground veal**
8 **ounces ground fresh pork**
1 **cup chopped onion**
1 **cup chopped celery with leaves**
¼ **cup snipped parsley**
1 **clove garlic, minced**

• • •

4 **beaten eggs**
¾ **cup grated Parmesan cheese**
1 **8-ounce package herb-seasoned stuffing mix**
1 **cup chicken broth**
½ **teaspoon rubbed sage**
1 **16- to 20-pound ready-to-cook turkey**
  Cooking oil

Cook frozen spinach according to package directions; drain and set aside. Cook sausage, ground veal, and ground pork till meat is done, about 15 minutes. (Break meat apart during cooking.) Stir in chopped onion, chopped celery, snipped parsley, and minced garlic; cover and cook 20 minutes longer. In mixing bowl combine beaten eggs, cooked spinach, and Parmesan cheese. In a large mixing bowl combine meat mixture, egg mixture, stuffing mix, chicken broth, and sage.

Stuff turkey with meat mixture; push legs under the band of skin at tail, or tie legs together and fasten to the tail. Place the bird, breast side up, on rack in shallow roasting pan. Rub skin with cooking oil. Insert a meat thermometer in center of inside thigh muscle, making sure the bulb does not touch bone. Cover bird loosely with foil.

Roast at 325° till meat thermometer registers 185° and the drumstick twists easily in the socket, 5½ to 6½ hours. During the last 45 minutes of roasting time, cut band of skin or string between legs and tail; uncover and continue roasting till done. Let stand 15 to 20 minutes before carving. To bake stuffing separately, turn stuffing mixture into a 2-quart casserole; bake at 325° for 1 hour. Serves 16 to 20.

Quick Limpa

1 cup all-purpose flour
1 cup rye flour
1½ teaspoons baking powder
1 teaspoon baking soda
1 teaspoon salt
¾ teaspoon caraway seed
• • •
1 beaten egg
1 cup milk
½ cup molasses
¼ cup butter *or* margarine, melted
1 tablespoon grated orange peel

In a large bowl stir together the flours, baking powder, baking soda, salt, and caraway seed. In another bowl combine egg, milk, molasses, melted butter, and orange peel. Add to dry ingredients and stir just enough to blend. Pour mixture into well-greased 8½x4½x2½-inch loaf pan. Bake at 325° for 40 minutes. Cover with foil and bake until top springs back when pressed lightly, 20 to 30 minutes longer. Remove from pan; cool on rack. Wrap and store overnight before serving. Makes 1 loaf.

Molasses-Pecan Bread

3 cups all-purpose flour
⅓ cup packed brown sugar
1 tablespoon baking powder
1 teaspoon ground cinnamon
½ teaspoon salt
¼ teaspoon baking soda
• • •
2 beaten eggs
1 cup milk
½ cup molasses
¼ cup cooking oil
½ cup chopped pecans

In a large bowl stir together thoroughly the flour, brown sugar, baking powder, cinnamon, salt, and baking soda. Stir together the eggs, milk, molasses, and oil; add to dry ingredients, mixing just enough to blend. Stir in the nuts. Turn batter into two greased 7½x3½x2-inch loaf pans. Bake at 325° for 50 to 55 minutes. Remove from pans; cool on rack. Wrap and store overnight before serving. Makes 2.

Inside-Outside Onion Bread

1 beaten egg
½ cup dairy sour cream
1 tablespoon instant minced onion
¼ teaspoon salt
½ cup milk
2 cups packaged biscuit mix
1 tablespoon snipped parsley

In a bowl combine egg, sour cream, onion, and salt; mix till well blended. Remove ⅓ cup sour cream mixture; set aside. Stir milk into remaining mixture. Add biscuit mix and parsley, stirring just till blended, about 30 seconds. Turn batter into greased 8½x4½x2½-inch loaf pan. Spread reserved sour cream mixture over batter. Bake at 325° till done, 35 to 40 minutes. Cool 10 minutes before removing from pan. Serve warm. Makes 1 loaf.

Raisin Brown Bread

1 cup raisins
1 beaten egg
1 cup packed brown sugar
2 tablespoons cooking oil
1 tablespoon grated orange peel
• • •
2½ cups all-purpose flour
2 teaspoons baking powder
1 teaspoon salt
½ teaspoon baking soda

Combine raisins and 1½ cups water; bring to boiling. Remove from heat; cool to room temperature. Stir in the egg, brown sugar, oil, and orange peel. Stir together the flour, baking powder, salt, and baking soda; add to the raisin mixture, stirring just till blended. Pour into a greased 8½x4½x2½-inch loaf pan. Bake at 325° till done, about 1 hour. Remove from pan and cool. Makes 1 loaf.

Baking chilled casseroles

Adjust baking times when starting with a chilled casserole. Allow 15 to 20 minutes of extra bake time.

Set the stage for an elaborate buffet dinner with a show-stopper! *Sherried Sweet Potato Bake* is studded with raisins and features a tart orange glaze. Select a colorful variety of crisp and chilled relishes to complement this hot and sweet vegetable casserole.

Shoestring Potatoes O'Brien

  1½ cups milk
  2 3-ounce packages cream cheese with
     chives, softened
  ¼ cup chopped green pepper
  ¼ cup chopped canned pimiento
  1 teaspoon salt
  ⅛ teaspoon pepper
  1 20-ounce package frozen shoestring
     potatoes, thawed
  ½ cup canned French-fried onions

Have milk at room temperature; gradually blend into cream cheese. Mix in next four ingredients. Stir in potatoes. Turn into 10x6x2-inch baking dish. Bake, covered, at 325° for 1 hour. Uncover; stir. Top with onions; bake 5 minutes longer. Makes 8 servings.

Potato-Onion au Gratin

  2 tablespoons margarine
  2 tablespoons all-
     purpose flour
  2 tablespoons dry onion soup mix
  1½ cups milk
  ¾ cup cheese spread
  6 cups thinly sliced potatoes

In saucepan melt margarine; blend in flour. Stir in soup mix. Stir in milk all at once; cook and stir till thickened and bubbly. Stir in cheese spread. Layer *half* the potatoes in 1½-quart casserole. Pour *half* the cheese sauce over potatoes; repeat. Cover; bake at 325° for 1 hour. Uncover; bake till potatoes are tender, about 30 minutes more. If desired, sprinkle with paprika. Makes 6 servings.

Candied Yam Boats

4 small yams *or* sweet potatoes
½ cup prepared mincemeat
3 tablespoons butter *or* margarine
1 tablespoon lemon juice
½ teaspoon salt
• • •
¼ cup chopped pecans

Scrub potatoes with a brush. Bake at 325° till tender, about 1 hour. Remove the potatoes from oven; cut in half lengthwise. Scoop out center of halves, leaving about ½-inch shell; set shells aside. In a mixing bowl mash centers; stir in mincemeat, butter or margarine, lemon juice, and salt. Sprinkle shells lightly with additional salt; spoon mashed potato mixture into potato shells. Sprinkle chopped pecans over tops of potatoes. Return to oven and bake at 325° till heated through, about 15 minutes longer. Makes 8 servings.

Sherried Sweet Potato Bake

These sparkly sweets make nice party fare —

8 medium sweet potatoes
1 cup packed brown sugar
2 tablespoons cornstarch
½ teaspoon salt
½ teaspoon shredded orange peel
2 cups orange juice
½ cup raisins
• • •
6 tablespoons butter *or* margarine
⅓ cup dry sherry
¼ cup chopped walnuts

Cook the sweet potatoes in boiling salted water till just tender; drain. Peel and cut lengthwise into ½-inch-thick slices. Arrange in 13x9x2-inch baking dish. Sprinkle with a little salt. In saucepan combine brown sugar, cornstarch, and the ½ teaspoon salt. Blend in orange peel and juice; add raisins. Cook and stir over medium heat till thickened and bubbly; cook 1 minute longer. Add butter or margarine, sherry, and walnuts, stirring till butter is melted. Pour over potatoes. Bake at 325° till potatoes are well glazed, about 30 minutes. Baste occasionally with orange juice mixture. Serves 8.

Oven Potato Salad

Canned potatoes make this easy —

½ cup dairy sour cream
½ cup mayonnaise *or* salad dressing
2 tablespoons sliced pimiento-
   stuffed green olives
1 teaspoon Italian seasoning
¼ teaspoon salt
⅛ teaspoon pepper
• • •
2 16-ounce cans sliced potatoes,
   or 1 29-ounce can sliced
   potatoes, drained
½ cup chopped onion
½ cup chopped green pepper
2 hard-cooked eggs, sliced

Combine sour cream, mayonnaise, olives, and seasonings. Stir in potatoes, onion, and green pepper. Turn into a 2-quart casserole. Bake, covered, at 325° about 40 minutes, stirring once. Stir before serving and garnish with egg slices. Makes 8 servings.

Sweet Potato Puff

An extra-easy vegetable soufflé —

¼ cup sliced green onion
2 tablespoons snipped parsley
¾ teaspoon salt
¼ teaspoon dried marjoram, crushed
   Dash pepper
3 tablespoons butter *or* margarine
• • •
3 tablespoons all-purpose flour
¾ cup milk
1½ cups mashed cooked sweet potatoes
3 egg yolks
3 stiffly beaten egg whites

In a saucepan cook onion, parsley, salt, marjoram, and pepper in butter or margarine till onion is tender but not brown. Blend in flour. Stir in the milk all at once; cook and stir till mixture is thickened and bubbly. Stir in sweet potatoes. Beat egg yolks till thick and lemon-colored, about 5 minutes. Slowly blend in sweet potato mixture. Fold into egg whites. Gently pour into a 1-quart soufflé dish. Bake at 325° for 60 to 65 minutes. Serves 5 or 6.

Cheesy Mashed Potatoes

2⅓ cups water
1 teaspoon instant minced onion
1 teaspoon dried parsley flakes
1 5-ounce package instant mashed
   potato buds
• • •
1 4-ounce container whipped cream
   cheese
1 beaten egg
1 tablespoon butter *or* margarine
   Paprika

In a saucepan heat water, minced onion, and parsley flakes. Use to prepare instant mashed potato buds according to package directions, *omitting butter.* Beat whipped cream cheese and egg into potatoes. Turn potatoes into a 1½-quart casserole; dot with butter or margarine and sprinkle with paprika. Bake at 325° for 30 to 35 minutes. (If desired, make casserole ahead; cover and refrigerate. Bake at 325° till heated through, about 1 hour.) Serves 8.

Calico Rice Bake

¾ cup water
1 tablespoon instant minced onion
¾ teaspoon salt
   Dash pepper
   Dash dried rosemary, crushed
¾ cup quick-cooking rice
1 cup shredded sharp Cheddar cheese
   (4 ounces)
1 5⅓-ounce can evaporated milk
3 beaten eggs
1 16-ounce can mixed vegetables,
   drained

In a medium saucepan combine the water, instant minced onion, salt, pepper, and rosemary; bring just to boiling. Stir in rice. Cover tightly; remove from heat and let stand 5 minutes. Fluff with a fork. Stir in the cheese, milk, and eggs. Stir in the drained vegetables. Turn rice-vegetable mixture into a 10x6x2-inch baking dish. Bake, uncovered, at 325° till a knife inserted halfway between the center and edge comes out clean, 25 to 30 minutes. Do not overbake. Makes 6 servings.

Baked Rice Amandine

2 teaspoons salt
1 cup long grain rice
⅓ cup butter *or* margarine
• • •
   Dash garlic salt
1 13¾-ounce can chicken broth *or* 2
   chicken bouillon cubes dissolved
   in 1¾ cups boiling water
2 tablespoons finely snipped parsley
¼ cup toasted slivered almonds

In saucepan combine salt and 2 cups water; bring to boiling and pour over rice. Let stand 30 minutes. Rinse rice with cold water; drain well. Melt butter in skillet. Add rice and cook over medium heat, stirring often, till butter is almost absorbed, about 5 minutes. Turn into 1-quart casserole; sprinkle with garlic salt. Pour broth over. Bake, covered, at 325° for 45 minutes. Stir in parsley. Sprinkle with slivered almonds. Bake, uncovered, 10 minutes longer. Makes 6 servings.

Eggplant Crunch Casserole

Zesty tomato sauce and crunchy corn chips are just right together in this eggplant dish—

1 small eggplant, peeled and cubed
   (1 pound)
1 cup chopped celery
½ cup chopped onion
½ cup chopped green pepper
¼ cup butter *or* margarine
• • •
1 8-ounce can tomato sauce
1 cup shredded sharp American cheese
   (4 ounces)
1 cup coarsely crushed corn chips

In a large skillet or saucepan cook eggplant, chopped celery, onion, and green pepper in butter or margarine till tender but not brown, about 15 minutes. Stir in the tomato sauce, cheese, and ¼ *cup* of the crushed corn chips. Turn eggplant mixture into a 1½-quart casserole. Bake, covered, at 325° till mixture is heated through, about 25 minutes. Stir lightly; top with a wreath of the remaining crushed corn chips. Bake 5 minutes. Serves 6 to 8.

Bean Pot Lentils

1 cup dry lentils (8 ounces)
1½ cups water
½ cup chopped onion
½ teaspoon salt
1 16-ounce can tomatoes, cut up
2 tablespoons packed brown sugar
1 tablespoon chili sauce
½ teaspoon dry mustard
2 slices bacon, diced

Rinse lentils; drain. In saucepan combine lentils, water, onion, and salt. Bring to boiling; cover and simmer 45 minutes. Stir in remaining ingredients. Turn mixture into 1½-quart bean pot or casserole. Bake, covered, at 325° for 1 hour. Uncover and stir; bake 30 minutes more. Stir before serving. Makes 6 servings.

Curried Vegetable-Cheese Bake

½ cup chopped onion
2 teaspoons curry powder
2 tablespoons butter *or* margarine
2 tablespoons all-purpose flour
¼ teaspoon salt
⅛ teaspoon pepper
1½ cups milk
1 cup shredded Swiss cheese
1 12-ounce can whole kernel corn with sweet peppers
1 tablespoon chopped canned green chili peppers
3 medium tomatoes, peeled and sliced
¾ cup soft bread crumbs
1 tablespoon butter, melted

Cook onion and curry powder in the 2 tablespoons butter till onion is tender but not brown. Blend in flour, salt, and pepper. Stir in milk all at once. Cook and stir till thickened and bubbly. Stir in cheese, corn, and chili peppers. Set aside. Arrange *half* the tomato slices in single layer in bottom of 10x6x2-inch baking dish. Pour *half* the corn mixture over tomatoes. Repeat with remaining tomato slices and corn mixture. Toss bread crumbs with melted butter. Sprinkle over casserole. Bake, uncovered, at 325° till heated through, 40 to 45 minutes. Makes 8 servings.

Carrot-Cheddar Casserole

Golden carrot casserole pictured on pages 38 and 39 is ideal for potluck dinners —

1 pound carrots, peeled and cut up
2 tablespoons butter *or* margarine
• • •
1½ cups milk
1 cup shredded Cheddar cheese (4 ounces)
¾ cup coarsely crushed saltine crackers
2 well beaten eggs
1 teaspoon salt

Cook carrots, covered, in small amount of boiling salted water for 15 to 20 minutes. Drain thoroughly. Stir butter or margarine into the carrots and mash coarsely with a fork. Combine the mashed carrots, milk, cheese, cracker crumbs, beaten eggs, and salt; mix well. Turn the carrot mixture into an 8x8x2-inch baking dish. Bake at 325° till a knife inserted just off-center comes out clean, 35 to 40 minutes. Makes 6 servings.

Baked Tomatoes and Cheese

Serve this accompaniment in salad bowls and call it a hot vegetable salad —

4 medium tomatoes, peeled
2 cups shredded sharp American cheese (8 ounces)
½ cup chopped onion
½ cup chopped green pepper
1 teaspoon sugar
¼ teaspoon pepper
½ cup crushed potato chips

Slice each tomato crosswise into fourths. Place *half* of the tomato slices in a single layer in a 10x6x2-inch baking dish. Sprinkle *half* of the cheese, *half* of the chopped onion, and *half* of the green pepper over tomato slices. Sprinkle with *half* the sugar and *half* the pepper. Repeat the layers of tomato, cheese, chopped onion, green pepper, sugar, and pepper. Cover and bake at 325° till vegetables are tender, about 30 minutes. Uncover and continue to bake about 10 minutes longer. Sprinkle with potato chips just before serving. Makes 6 servings.

Rhubaba

3 tablespoons butter *or* margarine
½ cup packed brown sugar
2 cups diced rhubarb (8 ounces)
¼ cup dry sherry
2 egg yolks
1 teaspoon lemon juice
⅔ cup granulated sugar
½ teaspoon vanilla
⅔ cup all-purpose flour
1 teaspoon baking powder
2 stiffly beaten egg whites

In oven melt butter in 8x1½-inch round baking dish; stir in brown sugar. Top with rhubarb. If desired, add few drops red food coloring to sherry; drizzle over rhubarb. In small mixing bowl beat egg yolks and lemon juice till thick and lemon-colored; gradually add granulated sugar and vanilla; beat till thick and light. Slowly stir in 3 tablespoons hot water. Stir together flour, baking powder, and ⅛ teaspoon salt; add to egg yolk mixture and stir to blend. Fold in egg whites; spoon over rhubarb. Bake at 325° till cake tests done, about 45 minutes. Remove from oven; let stand 5 minutes. Loosen sides; invert onto serving plate. Serve warm with sweetened whipped cream, if desired. Makes 6 to 8 servings.

Choco-Peanut Butter Bars

2 rolls refrigerated peanut butter
    cookie dough
1 6-ounce package semisweet chocolate
    pieces

Break cookie dough into 1-inch pieces. Softening with hands, press *half* of dough evenly into an ungreased 13x9x2-inch baking pan. Sprinkle with chocolate pieces. Press remaining dough over chocolate pieces. Bake at 325° till set, about 40 minutes. Makes 36 bars.

◀ **Tonight, offer** a noticeably different dessert. *Rhubaba* features a golden cake topped with sherry-sparked fruit. For a decorative touch, arrange almonds and fruit peels atop.

Spiced Apple Upside-Down Cake

1 14-ounce jar spiced apple rings
¼ cup butter *or* margarine, melted
½ cup packed brown sugar
½ cup granulated sugar
⅓ cup shortening
1 teaspoon vanilla
1 egg
1 cup all-purpose flour
1½ teaspoons baking powder
½ cup milk
    Cinnamon Sauce

Drain spiced apple rings, reserving syrup. In 8x8x2-inch baking dish combine butter, brown sugar, and *2 tablespoons* of the reserved syrup. Arrange apple rings in bottom of baking dish. Cream together granulated sugar, shortening, and vanilla. Add egg; beat well. Stir together thoroughly the flour, baking powder, and ¼ teaspoon salt; add to creamed mixture alternately with milk, beating after each addition. Spread batter over apple rings. Bake at 325° till cake tests done, 40 to 45 minutes. Cool 5 minutes; invert on plate. Serve warm with Cinnamon Sauce. Serves 6 to 8.

Cinnamon Sauce: Add enough water to remaining spiced apple syrup to make ¾ cup. In saucepan combine 2 tablespoons granulated sugar and 1 tablespoon cornstarch; stir in spiced apple syrup. Cook and stir till thickened and bubbly. Stir in 1 teaspoon lemon juice.

Baked Rice Pudding

3 beaten eggs
2 cups milk
½ cup sugar
1 teaspoon vanilla
1¾ to 2 cups cooked long grain rice
⅓ to ½ cup raisins (optional)
    Ground nutmeg

Combine first 4 ingredients and ½ teaspoon salt. Stir in rice and raisins. Turn into 10x6x2-inch baking dish. Bake, uncovered, at 325° for 30 minutes; stir. Sprinkle with nutmeg. Bake till knife inserted halfway between center and edge comes out clean, about 30 minutes. Makes 6 servings.

Brandy-Sauced Bread Pudding

12 slices white bread
4 eggs
3 cups milk
1 16-ounce can applesauce
1 cup sugar
2 tablespoons butter, melted
2 teaspoons vanilla
1 teaspoon ground cinnamon
Brandy Sauce

Slice bread into ½-inch-wide strips. Combine eggs, milk, applesauce, sugar, butter, vanilla, cinnamon, and ½ teaspoon salt. Arrange *one-third* of the bread strips in a single layer in 11x7x2-inch baking pan. Top with *half* of the applesauce mixture. Repeat layers of bread and applesauce mixture. Top with remaining bread. Bake at 325° till center is set, about 1 hour. Serve with Brandy Sauce. Serves 8.

Brandy Sauce: Separate 1 egg; beat the egg white till soft peaks form. Gradually add 2 tablespoons sugar, beating till stiff peaks form. Beat egg yolk slightly; add to egg white, beating till mixed. Whip 1 cup whipping cream; fold into egg mixture. Stir in ⅓ cup brandy. Serve over pudding.

Vermont Indian Pudding

COST-CUTTING RECIPE

1½ cups milk
¼ cup yellow cornmeal
1 beaten egg
¼ cup maple-flavored syrup
¼ cup raisins
2 tablespoons sugar
1 tablespoon margarine *or* butter
¼ teaspoon ground ginger
¼ teaspoon ground cinnamon

In a saucepan combine milk and cornmeal. Cook and stir over moderate heat till thick, about 10 minutes. Remove from heat. In a bowl combine the egg, maple-flavored syrup, raisins, sugar, margarine or butter, ginger, and cinnamon. Stir in the cornmeal mixture. Turn into a 20-ounce casserole. Bake, uncovered, at 300° till just set, 60 to 70 minutes. Serve warm with light cream or vanilla ice cream, if desired. Makes 4 servings.

Pineapple Tapioca Pudding

A tangy finale to an oriental meal—

1 20-ounce can pineapple chunks
    (juice pack)
¾ cup hot water
½ cup sugar
3 tablespoons quick-cooking tapioca
1 tablespoon lemon juice
½ teaspoon salt
    Dash ground nutmeg
    Frozen whipped dessert topping,
    thawed
½ cup chopped walnuts

In a bowl combine undrained pineapple, hot water, sugar, tapioca, lemon juice, salt, and nutmeg. Let stand 10 minutes. Pour into a 1-quart casserole. Bake, uncovered, at 325° till tapioca granules are clear and pudding is thick, 40 to 50 minutes, stirring occasionally. Cool slightly. Serve topped with whipped dessert topping and sprinkled with chopped walnuts. Makes 6 servings.

Baked Orange Tapioca

Using your oven is an easy way to prepare this fresh fruit tapioca pudding—

2 medium oranges
    Orange juice (about 1 cup)
¼ cup sugar
¼ cup water
3 tablespoons quick-cooking tapioca
⅛ teaspoon salt
⅛ teaspoon ground ginger
4 marshmallows

Section the oranges over a small bowl to catch the juice; halve the orange sections. To reserved juice add enough additional orange juice to make 1¼ cups juice. Combine the orange sections, orange juice, sugar, water, tapioca, salt, and ginger.

Turn mixture into a 1-quart casserole. Let stand for 10 minutes. Bake, uncovered, at 325° till tapioca granules are clear and pudding is thick, 40 to 45 minutes, stirring occasionally. Top with marshmallows. Return to oven till marshmallows are golden, about 5 minutes. Makes 4 servings.

Cherry-Coconut Delight

¾ cup flaked coconut
¾ cup all-purpose flour
⅓ cup packed brown sugar
⅓ cup finely crushed saltine crackers
    (9 crackers)
6 tablespoons butter *or* margarine,
    melted
• • •
1 21-ounce can cherry pie filling
  Whipped cream

In a bowl combine flaked coconut, flour, brown sugar, and crushed crackers; stir in butter and mix well. Press *two-thirds* of the mixture into a 9-inch pie plate. Spread with cherry pie filling. Sprinkle remaining crumb mixture atop fruit. Bake at 325° till topping is golden, about 25 minutes. Serve warm. Garnish with dollops of whipped cream. Makes 6 servings.

Brazilian Custards

Zesty orange peel, coffee, and fudge topping harmonize for sophisticated flavor—

2 tablespoons fudge topping
4 beaten eggs
½ cup sugar
2 teaspoons instant coffee crystals
½ teaspoon salt
½ teaspoon grated orange peel
½ teaspoon vanilla
  Dash ground nutmeg
2½ cups milk

Spoon *1 teaspoon* fudge topping into the bottom of *each* of six 6-ounce custard cups*; set aside. In mixing bowl combine eggs, sugar, instant coffee crystals, salt, orange peel, vanilla, and nutmeg. Stir in milk. Pour the mixture carefully over fudge topping. Set custard cups in shallow baking pan on oven rack. Pour hot water around custard cups in pan to a depth of 1 inch. Bake at 325° till knife inserted just off-center comes out clean, 40 to 45 minutes. Makes 6 servings.
    *Note: Or, use a 1-quart casserole. Spread fudge topping in bottom of casserole. Carefully pour custard mixture over topping. Bake in pan of hot water at 325° for 50 minutes.

Double-Decker Pumpkin Pudding

A cake and pudding dessert with flavor reminiscent of home-style pumpkin pie—

1 16-ounce can pumpkin
¾ cup sugar
1 5⅓-ounce can evaporated milk
2 eggs
¼ cup butter *or* margarine, melted
1 teaspoon pumpkin pie spice
• • •
½ cup finely chopped pecans
1 package 1-layer-size spice cake mix
  Whipped cream (optional)

In a large mixing bowl combine pumpkin, sugar, milk, eggs, butter or margarine, and pumpkin pie spice. Beat till well combined. Fold in pecans; pour into greased 13x9x2-inch baking pan. Prepare cake mix according to package directions. Spread cake batter over pumpkin mixture. Bake, uncovered, at 325° till cake tests done, about 45 minutes. If desired, top with whipped cream. Makes 12 servings.

Puffy Butterscotch Custards

Enjoy the soufflé-like texture of this dessert—

¼ cup butter *or* margarine
¾ cup packed brown sugar
¼ teaspoon salt
• • •
1¾ cups milk, scalded
3 beaten egg yolks
1 teaspoon vanilla
• • •
3 stiffly beaten egg whites
⅓ cup chopped walnuts *or* pecans

Cream together butter or margarine, brown sugar, and salt till mixture is light and fluffy. Gradually blend the hot milk into beaten egg yolks. Stir in vanilla. Add to creamed mixture, blending thoroughly. Fold in the stiffly beaten egg whites. Pour the mixture into six 6-ounce custard cups; top with chopped walnuts or pecans. Set cups in a shallow pan on oven rack. Pour hot water around cups in pan to a depth of 1 inch. Bake at 325° till a knife inserted just off-center comes out clean, about 45 minutes. Serve warm or chilled. Serves 6.

Moderate oven dishes

Food dishes particularly suited to this temperature range (350° to 375° F.) include meat loaves, casseroles, and desserts. You'll find a number of these and other dishes in this recipe section. Select compatible foods for a meal and then bake them together in the oven.

Orange-Glazed Spareribs

    4 pounds pork spareribs
    1 6-ounce can frozen orange juice
       concentrate, thawed
    1½ teaspoons Worcestershire sauce
    ½ teaspoon garlic salt
    ⅛ teaspoon pepper

In large kettle or Dutch oven cover ribs with salted water. Cover kettle; simmer till ribs are almost tender, about 1 hour. Drain thoroughly. Meanwhile, in bowl combine remaining ingredients. Place ribs in shallow roasting pan; brush with sauce. Roast at 350° till ribs are glazed and browned, 30 to 40 minutes; baste occasionally with sauce. Makes 4 servings.

Saucy Ham Slices

    1 10¾-ounce can condensed tomato
       soup
    ¼ cup chopped onion
    2 tablespoons sweet pickle relish
    1 tablespoon packed brown sugar
    1 tablespoon vinegar
    1 tablespoon Worcestershire sauce
    1 teaspoon prepared horseradish
    2 slices fully cooked ham, cut ½ inch
       thick (2 pounds)
    1 20-ounce can pie-sliced apples,
       drained

Combine first 7 ingredients; set aside. Place one ham slice in 12x7½x2-inch baking dish; top with *half* the apple slices. Cover with *half* the soup mixture. Repeat layers. Cover and heat in a 350° oven for 45 minutes; uncover and cook till heated through, 10 to 15 minutes more. Makes 8 servings.

Pork Chop-Pear Bake

    6 pork loin chops, cut ¾ inch thick
    2 tablespoons all-purpose flour
    2 tablespoons cooking oil
    1 14-ounce jar spiced pear halves
       Ground nutmeg

Trim fat from chops. Coat chops with mixture of the flour, ¾ teaspoon salt, and dash pepper. Brown chops on both sides in hot oil. Place chops in 12x7½x2-inch baking dish. Drain pears; reserve ½ cup syrup. Set pears aside. Pour reserved syrup over meat. Cover; place in a 350° oven for 45 minutes. Add pears; sprinkle with nutmeg. Cook till heated through, 10 to 15 minutes more. Serves 6.

Glazed Canadian-Style Bacon

    1 3-pound piece Canadian-style bacon
    ½ cup packed brown sugar
    1 tablespoon all-purpose flour
    ½ teaspoon dry mustard
    ⅛ teaspoon ground cloves
    2 tablespoons water

Place bacon in shallow baking pan. Bake, uncovered, at 350° for 1 hour. Meanwhile, blend together next 4 ingredients; mix in water. Brush *half* the mixture on bacon; return to oven for 10 minutes. Brush on remaining mixture; bake 5 minutes more. Serves 12.

Tangy sauce adds a great taste sensation to ▶ *Orange-Glazed Spareribs.* For a change of flavor, use a different frozen fruit juice concentrate such as pineapple or lemonade.

Curried Chinese Pork

Mix 1 teaspoon salt and ½ teaspoon curry powder; rub into one 4-pound pork shoulder roast. In Dutch oven brown the meat in small amount of hot cooking oil; add ½ cup water. Cover and place in a 350° oven for 1 hour; drain. Combine one 16-ounce can fancy mixed Chinese vegetables, drained; one 10¾-ounce can condensed cream of mushroom soup; ¾ cup water; ½ cup long grain rice; 1½ teaspoons curry powder; ½ teaspoon salt; and ⅛ teaspoon pepper. Pour around meat. Cover; cook till meat and rice are tender, about 1½ hours.

To serve, place meat on platter; surround with vegetables. Pass soy sauce. Serves 8.

Scotch Eggs

    1 pound bulk pork sausage
    8 hard-cooked eggs
    ½ cup fine dry bread crumbs
    ¼ teaspoon paprika
    1 beaten egg

On lightly floured surface flatten sausage to 8x8-inch square; cut in 8 pieces. Mold *each* piece around 1 egg, completely covering egg. Combine bread crumbs and paprika. Dip meat-covered eggs in beaten egg, then in crumb mixture. Place in shallow baking pan. Bake at 375° for 20 to 25 minutes. Garnish with parsley, if desired. Makes 8 servings.

Pork-Stuffed Enchiladas

Combine 1½ cups cubed cooked pork, ½ cup shredded sharp Cheddar cheese, and ½ cup chopped onion; set aside. In saucepan heat one 10¾-ounce can condensed cream of mushroom soup, one 10¾-ounce can condensed tomato soup, and one 10-ounce can mild enchilada sauce to boiling. Quickly dip 12 frozen tortillas, thawed, in sauce. Divide meat mixture among tortillas; roll up. Place in 12x7½x2-inch baking dish. Top with remaining sauce and sprinkle with an additional ½ cup shredded sharp Cheddar cheese. Bake at 350° for 25 to 30 minutes. Makes 6 servings.

Pork Stuffing Casserole

    1 6-ounce package chicken-flavored
      stuffing mix
    2 beaten eggs
    1 10¾-ounce can condensed cream of
      mushroom soup
    1 teaspoon instant chicken bouillon
      granules
    ¼ cup butter *or* margarine
    2 cups diced cooked pork
    ½ cup milk
    2 tablespoons chopped canned pimiento

Combine crumb portion of stuffing mix with eggs and *half* the soup; set aside. In saucepan combine seasoning portion of stuffing mix with bouillon granules, butter, and 1 cup water; bring to boiling. Stir in crumb mixture; mix well. Spread in 2-quart casserole; top with diced pork. In another bowl combine remaining soup, milk, and pimiento. Pour over pork and stuffing mixture. Bake, covered, at 350° till set, about 45 minutes. Garnish with green pepper rings, if desired. Serves 6.

Stuffed Pepper Cups

    6 medium green peppers
    1 10½-ounce can condensed beef broth
    1 soup can water (1⅓ cups)
    1 cup long grain rice
    ½ cup finely chopped onion
    ¼ cup chopped celery
    3 tablespoons butter *or* margarine
    1½ cups diced fully cooked ham
    1 cup soft bread crumbs (1½ slices)

Cut tops from peppers; remove seeds and membranes. Chop tops to make ⅓ cup; set aside. Cook peppers in boiling water 5 minutes; drain. Heat broth, water, rice, and ½ teaspoon salt to boiling; stir. Cover and cook over very low heat 15 minutes. Cook the ⅓ cup chopped green pepper, onion, and celery in *2 tablespoons* butter till tender. Stir in ham. Add to rice mixture; toss lightly to mix. Spoon into peppers. Melt remaining butter; combine with crumbs. Sprinkle over tops of peppers. Place in 12x7½x2-inch baking dish. Bake at 350° for 20 to 25 minutes. Serves 6.

Mexican Flank Steak

　2 beef flank steaks (2 pounds)
　½ teaspoon salt
　⅛ teaspoon garlic salt
　1 15-ounce can tamales in sauce
　1 beef bouillon cube
　¼ cup boiling water
　1 8-ounce can tomato sauce
　　Dash bottled hot pepper sauce

Pound the meat on both sides; sprinkle with salt, garlic salt, and ⅛ teaspoon pepper. Unwrap tamales; place in bowl. Break up tamales slightly with fork; spread over steaks. Roll up each steak jelly-roll fashion; tie closed. Place in shallow baking pan. Dissolve bouillon cube in boiling water; combine with tomato sauce and hot pepper sauce. Pour mixture over meat. Place in a 350° oven for 1¼ to 1½ hours; baste often. Serves 6 to 8.

Spanish Rice Roast

Trim excess fat from a 3-pound beef chuck roast. Season meat with salt and pepper; place in center of long piece of wide foil. Combine 1½ cups tomato juice; one 6-ounce package Spanish rice mix; one 3-ounce can sliced mushrooms, drained; ½ cup water; 1 tablespoon snipped parsley; ½ teaspoon salt; and dash pepper. Spoon mixture around roast. Seal foil. Place foil packet on rack in shallow roasting pan. Place in a 350° oven till meat is tender, about 2½ hours. Serves 6.

Spanish Meatballs

　1½ pounds ground beef
　½ cup long grain rice
　½ cup chopped onion
　½ cup chopped green pepper
　½ teaspoon salt
　1 10¾-ounce can condensed tomato soup
　1 soup can water (1⅓ cups)

Combine first 5 ingredients. Shape into 24 balls; place in 2-quart casserole. Blend soup and water; pour over meatballs. Bake, covered, at 350° for 1½ hours. Serves 6.

Sweet Pickle Meat Loaf

　2 beaten eggs
　1 cup soft bread crumbs
　¼ cup catsup
　¼ cup finely chopped onion
　2 tablespoons sweet pickle relish
　1 tablespoon prepared mustard
　1 teaspoon prepared horseradish
1½ pounds ground beef
　¼ cup catsup

Combine first 7 ingredients and 1 teaspoon salt; add beef and mix well. Shape into 9x4-inch loaf, place in 10x6x2-inch baking dish. Bake at 350° for 1 hour. Spread with ¼ cup catsup. Bake 15 minutes more. Serves 6 to 8.

Dilly Meat Loaf

In large bowl combine 2 beaten eggs, ½ cup dairy sour cream, 1 cup soft bread crumbs, ¼ cup chopped onion, 2 tablespoons chopped canned pimiento, 1 teaspoon salt, and 1 teaspoon dried dillweed; add 1½ pounds ground beef and mix well. Place mixture in an 8½x4½x2½-inch loaf pan. Bake at 350° about 1¼ hours. Makes 6 to 8 servings.

Gingersnap Meat Loaf

　2 beaten eggs
　¼ cup milk
　½ cup coarsely crushed gingersnaps
　¼ cup finely chopped onion
　1 tablespoon red wine vinegar
1½ pounds ground beef
　　Gingersnap Sauce

In large bowl combine first 5 ingredients, 1 teaspoon salt, and dash pepper. Add ground beef and mix well. Place in an 8½x4½x2½-inch loaf pan. Bake at 350° about 1¼ hours. Serve with Gingersnap Sauce. Serves 6.

Gingersnap Sauce: In saucepan mix ¾ cup canned condensed beef broth, ⅓ cup crushed gingersnaps, ⅓ cup packed brown sugar, ¼ cup raisins, 3 tablespoons vinegar, and 3 tablespoons water. Bring to boiling; reduce heat. Cook and stir till smooth, about 1 minute.

Corned Beef Balls in Rice Ring

Mix 2 beaten eggs, ¼ cup milk, ½ cup fine dry bread crumbs, and two 12-ounce cans corned beef, flaked. Form into 1-inch balls. Bake in greased 15½x10½x2-inch baking pan at 350° for 20 minutes. Cook 1⅓ cups long grain rice according to package directions; stir in 2 tablespoons butter. Stir in one 10-ounce package frozen mixed vegetables, cooked and drained. Press into greased 5½-cup ring mold. Unmold; fill center with meatballs. Mix one 11-ounce can condensed Cheddar cheese soup and ⅓ cup milk; heat through. Drizzle over meat and rice. Serves 8.

Western Hamburger Pie

  ½ **cup boiling water**
  ⅓ **cup yellow cornmeal**
  2 **teaspoons butter** *or* **margarine**
  2 **sticks piecrust mix, crumbled**
• • •
  1 **pound ground beef**
  1 **cup chopped onion**
  ¼ **cup chopped green pepper**
  2 **tablespoons all-purpose flour**
  ¾ **teaspoon salt**
  ⅛ **teaspoon pepper**
  1 **beaten egg**
  1 **cup dairy sour cream**
  2 **tablespoons snipped parsley**

In bowl stir together first 3 ingredients; set aside for 15 minutes to soften cornmeal. Add piecrust mix; stir till dough holds together. Roll out *half* the dough and line a 9-inch pie plate with it; flute edges. Cover remaining pastry; set aside for topper.

In skillet cook beef, onion, and green pepper till meat is browned and vegetables are tender. Drain off fat. Stir in flour, salt, and pepper; cook 2 minutes more. Remove from heat. Combine egg, sour cream, and parsley; add to meat mixture, mixing thoroughly. Turn into crust-lined pie plate. Roll out remaining pastry to 8-inch circle. Cut in 6 pie-shaped wedges. Prick with fork. Place atop meat pie. Bake at 375° till pastry is lightly browned, 45 to 50 minutes. Cut into wedges to serve; top each with warmed catsup, if desired. Serves 6.

Shortcut Pastitsio

Cook ½ pound lean ground beef and ½ cup chopped onion till beef is browned and onion is tender. Stir in ¼ cup snipped parsley; 1 teaspoon salt; ½ teaspoon dried basil, crushed; dash pepper; and dash ground cinnamon. Stir in one 15-ounce can tomato sauce, 1 cup water, and ⅔ cup uncooked elbow macaroni. Bring to boiling; cover. Reduce heat; cook till macaroni is tender, 15 to 20 minutes, stirring often. Stir in ½ cup shredded sharp American cheese. Turn into 1½-quart casserole.

In saucepan stir 4 teaspoons all-purpose flour and ¼ teaspoon dry mustard into 2 tablespoons melted butter *or* margarine. Add 1⅓ cups milk; cook and stir over low heat till thickened and bubbly. Stir some of hot mixture into 2 beaten eggs; return to saucepan. Cook and stir over low heat 2 minutes. Pour sauce over mixture in casserole. Bake at 350° till top is set, 30 to 35 minutes. Let stand 5 minutes before serving. Makes 4 servings.

Noodles 'n Cheeseburgers

COST-CUTTING RECIPE

  4 **lasagne noodles**
  1 **pound ground beef**
  ½ **teaspoon Worcestershire sauce**
  ¼ **cup chopped onion**
  ¼ **cup chopped green pepper**
  2 **tablespoons margarine** *or* **butter**
  2 **tablespoons all-purpose flour**
  1 **cup milk**
  4 **slices sharp American cheese**

Cook noodles in boiling salted water 20 minutes; drain. Combine beef, Worcestershire, and ½ teaspoon salt; mix well. Shape into 6 thin patties; brown in skillet. Remove patties; drain off fat. In skillet cook onion and green pepper in margarine till tender. Blend in flour and ½ teaspoon salt. Add milk all at once; cook and stir till thickened. Cut *3 slices* cheese into small pieces. In 10x6x2-inch baking dish layer 2 noodles, *half* the sauce, and *half* the cut-up cheese. Repeat layers. Top with meat patties. Bake at 350° for 20 minutes. Cut remaining cheese slice into 6 triangles; place one atop each patty. Bake 2 minutes more. Makes 4 to 6 servings.

Macaroni Shells Florentine

　20 jumbo macaroni shells
　½ cup finely chopped celery
　2 tablespoons chopped onion
　1 tablespoon cooking oil
　2 cups cream-style cottage cheese
　1 10-ounce package frozen chopped
　　　spinach, cooked and drained
　1 beaten egg
　½ teaspoon salt
　⅛ teaspoon dried oregano, crushed
　⅛ teaspoon ground nutmeg
　　　Dash pepper
　　　• • •
　　　Parmesan Sauce

Cook the macaroni shells according to package directions; drain and set aside. Cook celery and onion in hot oil till tender but not brown; drain. Combine cooked celery and onion, cottage cheese, cooked spinach, egg, salt, oregano, nutmeg, and pepper; mix well. Fill macaroni shells with spinach mixture.

Prepare Parmesan Sauce; pour *half* the sauce into bottom of a 12x7½x2-inch baking dish. Arrange stuffed macaroni shells in the cheese sauce in the baking dish. Cover with foil; bake at 375° for 20 minutes. Pour remaining Parmesan Sauce over shells. Bake, uncovered, 15 minutes longer. Sprinkle with grated Parmesan cheese, if desired. Serves 8 to 10.

Parmesan Sauce: In saucepan cook 2 tablespoons chopped onion in 3 tablespoons hot cooking oil till tender but not brown; blend in 3 tablespoons all-purpose flour, ¼ teaspoon salt, and dash pepper. Stir in 1½ cups milk and ¾ cup chicken broth. Cook, stirring constantly, until sauce is thickened and bubbly. Stir in ¼ cup grated Parmesan cheese.

Costly ingredients aren't necessary for an exotic foreign main dish. *Macaroni Shells Florentine* is a meatless casserole featuring jumbo macaroni shells stuffed with a chopped spinach-cottage cheese mixture. Extra flavor comes from a creamy Parmesan Sauce.

Prepare an easy oven meal by using *Cherry Chicken* (recipe on page 65) or *Saucy Halibut Steaks* as the main dish. Canned pie filling adds flavor and color to the chicken, and the fish becomes an elegant entrée when garnished with lime slices and mint sprigs.

Saucy Halibut Steaks

    4 fresh *or* frozen halibut steaks
    1 beaten egg
    1 10½-ounce can condensed cream of
        celery soup
    ¼ cup milk
    ¼ cup grated Parmesan cheese
    3 tablespoons fine dry bread crumbs
    1 tablespoon butter, melted

Thaw frozen fish. Place fish in 11x7½x1½-inch baking pan. In saucepan combine egg, soup, milk, and *half* the Parmesan cheese. Stir over low heat till cheese melts. Pour over fish. Toss bread crumbs with melted butter and remaining cheese. Sprinkle atop fish. Bake at 375° till fish flakes easily when tested with a fork, 20 to 25 minutes. Makes 8 servings.

Nutty Tuna-Noodle Bake

    4 ounces medium noodles (2 cups)
    1 10¾-ounce can condensed cream of
        mushroom soup
    ¼ cup dry white wine
    ¼ cup water
    1 6½- or 7-ounce can tuna, drained
    2 tablespoons chopped canned pimiento
    ½ cup coarsely chopped cashew nuts

Cook noodles in boiling salted water till nearly tender, about 8 minutes; drain well. Combine soup, wine, and water. Flake tuna; fold into soup mixture with noodles and pimiento. Turn into 1½-quart casserole. Sprinkle cashews over mixture. Bake, uncovered, at 350° till heated through, 30 to 35 minutes. Makes 4 servings.

Tuna Puff

¼ cup margarine *or* butter
¼ cup all-purpose flour
½ teaspoon prepared mustard
¼ teaspoon salt
1 cup milk
4 beaten egg yolks
1 6½- or 7-ounce can tuna, drained
3 tablespoons chopped canned pimiento
4 stiffly beaten egg whites
Easy Cheese Sauce

In medium saucepan melt margarine. Stir in flour, mustard, and salt; add milk. Cook and stir till mixture thickens and bubbles. Stir moderate amount of hot mixture into beaten egg yolks; return to saucepan. Cook and stir 2 minutes more. Flake tuna; stir into sauce with pimiento. Cool slightly. Fold egg whites into tuna mixture. Turn into *ungreased* 5-cup soufflé dish or casserole. Bake at 375° till puffy and golden, 35 to 40 minutes. Serve with Easy Cheese Sauce. Makes 4 servings.

Easy Cheese Sauce: In saucepan blend together one 11-ounce can condensed Cheddar cheese soup and ¼ cup milk; heat.

Shrimp and Stuffing Bake

½ cup chopped celery
½ cup chopped onion
2 tablespoons butter *or* margarine
1 10½-ounce can condensed cream of shrimp soup
¼ cup snipped parsley
¼ cup milk
½ teaspoon ground sage
¼ teaspoon dried thyme, crushed
2 beaten eggs
4 cups dry French bread cubes
2 4½-ounce cans shrimp, drained

In 3-quart saucepan cook celery and onion in butter till tender. Stir in soup, parsley, milk, sage, thyme, and dash pepper. Add eggs, bread cubes, and shrimp; mix well. Turn into 1½-quart casserole. Bake, covered, at 350° for 30 minutes. Uncover; bake 10 minutes more. Garnish with additional shrimp and parsley, if desired. Makes 5 servings.

Shrimp and Green Bean Bake

1 4½-ounce can shrimp, drained
1 9-ounce package frozen French-style green beans
1 10½-ounce can condensed cream of celery soup
2 tablespoons snipped parsley
¼ teaspoon grated lemon peel
1 teaspoon lemon juice
½ cup shredded American cheese
Paprika

Thoroughly rinse shrimp. Cook beans following package directions, omitting the salt; drain well. Place beans in 8x1½-inch round baking dish. Cover with shrimp. Combine soup, parsley, lemon peel, and juice; pour over shrimp. Cover and bake at 350° for 15 minutes. Uncover and top with cheese. Sprinkle with paprika. Bake till cheese melts, 5 to 10 minutes more. Makes 4 or 5 servings.

Baked Stuffed Salmon

1½ cups sliced fresh mushrooms
1 cup shredded carrot
¼ cup sliced green onion
¼ cup snipped parsley
¼ cup butter *or* margarine
1 6-ounce package long grain and wild rice mix
1½ cups chicken broth
1 cup water
⅛ teaspoon pepper
1 6-pound dressed salmon
3 tablespoons butter, melted

In saucepan cook mushrooms, carrot, onion, and parsley in ¼ cup butter till tender. Add rice and seasonings from mix; stir to combine. Add broth, water, and pepper. Cover; cook over low heat till rice is tender and liquid is absorbed, about 20 minutes. Remove head of fish, if desired. Rinse fish and pat dry. Place in greased 15½x10½x1-inch baking pan. Brush melted butter on inside and outside of fish; sprinkle fish cavity with salt and pepper. Stuff loosely with rice mixture. Bake, covered, at 350° till fish flakes easily when tested with a fork, about 1¼ hours. Makes 12 servings.

Chicken Oahu

Combine 4 cups herb-seasoned stuffing cubes and one 13¼-ounce can crushed pineapple, *undrained*. Place in greased 13x9x2-inch baking pan. Coat one 2½- to 3-pound ready-to-cook broiler-fryer chicken, cut up, with mixture of ½ cup all-purpose flour, ½ teaspoon salt, ½ teaspoon paprika, and dash pepper. In skillet brown the chicken in ¼ cup hot cooking oil. Place chicken atop stuffing. Cover with foil. Bake at 375° till chicken is tender, 50 to 60 minutes.

Combine 1½ cups finely chopped celery, ½ cup finely chopped onion, ½ cup water, and 2 tablespoons finely chopped green pepper. Cover; simmer till tender, 12 to 15 minutes. Add one 10¾-ounce can condensed cream of mushroom soup, ½ cup dairy sour cream, and 1 tablespoon soy sauce; heat through *(do not boil)*. Spoon over chicken. Serves 6.

Saucy Chicken Squares

2 cups soft bread crumbs
2 cups chicken broth
4 beaten eggs
⅓ cup chopped celery
¼ cup chopped canned pimiento
2 tablespoons finely chopped onion
½ teaspoon salt
¼ teaspoon poultry seasoning
3 cups chopped cooked chicken
1 cup cooked long grain rice
Mushroom Sauce

Combine first 8 ingredients. Stir in chicken and rice. Bake in 9x9x2-inch baking pan at 350° for 45 to 50 minutes. Cut in squares; serve with Mushroom Sauce. Makes 8 servings.

Mushroom Sauce: In saucepan blend one 10¾-ounce can condensed cream of mushroom soup and ¼ cup milk; heat through.

This Polynesian-inspired main dish features a pineapple stuffing that you can also use as a side dish. Team easy-to-make *Chicken Oahu* with vegetable, salad, and dessert for a low-cost meal that is sure to get compliments from your family or guests.

Cherry Chicken

Colorful low-cost main dish that's pictured on page 62—

3 tablespoons margarine
1 2- to 2½-pound ready-to-cook
   broiler-fryer chicken, cut up
¼ cup all-purpose flour
1 teaspoon salt
¼ teaspoon paprika
¼ teaspoon pepper
1 21-ounce can cherry pie filling
½ cup dry white wine
¼ cup packed brown sugar
½ teaspoon salt
¼ teaspoon ground nutmeg
¼ teaspoon ground allspice
¼ teaspoon ground cloves

In 12x7½x2-inch baking dish melt margarine in oven at 375°. Meanwhile, coat chicken with mixture of flour, 1 teaspoon salt, paprika, and pepper. Place chicken in baking dish. Bake at 375° for 40 minutes, turning once after 20 minutes. In saucepan heat remaining ingredients; pour over chicken. Continue baking till chicken is done, about 30 minutes more. Skim off excess fat. Makes 4 servings.

Turkey-Almond Casserole

1 8-ounce package frozen mixed
   vegetables in onion sauce
   Milk
1 6-ounce package noodles with
   chicken-almond mix
2⅓ cups boiling water
1½ to 2 cups cubed cooked turkey
2 tablespoons butter *or* margarine
½ cup crushed potato chips

Prepare vegetables following package directions, *except use milk*. Combine vegetables with noodles from chicken-almond mix, packet of noodle sauce from the mix, boiling water, turkey, and butter; mix well. Pour into 1½-quart casserole. Cover; bake at 375° for 25 minutes. Uncover and stir well. Sprinkle with potato chips and almonds from the mix; bake 5 to 10 minutes more. Let stand 5 minutes before serving. Makes 4 servings.

Capon with Mushroom Stuffing

Pecans are a crunchy texture surprise—

In saucepan cook 1½ cups sliced fresh mushrooms; 1⅓ cups quick-cooking rice; ¼ cup chopped onion; ¼ cup snipped celery leaves; 1½ teaspoons salt; ¼ teaspoon dried oregano, crushed; ¼ teaspoon rubbed sage; ¼ teaspoon dried thyme, crushed; and dash pepper in ¼ cup butter *or* margarine till vegetables are tender. Stir in 1½ cups water. Bring to boiling. Reduce heat and simmer, uncovered, till most of the water is absorbed, 6 to 8 minutes; stir once or twice. Remove from heat. Add ⅓ cup chopped pecans; mix lightly.

Rinse a 5- to 7-pound ready-to-cook capon; pat dry and salt inside. Stuff bird with mushroom mixture; push drumsticks under band of skin at tail, or tie to tail. Place, breast side up, on rack in shallow roasting pan. Rub skin with cooking oil. Roast, uncovered, at 375° till meat thermometer registers 185°, about 2 hours. Serves 6 to 8.

Apricot Chicken in Wine Sauce

1 2½- to 3-pound ready-to-cook
   broiler-fryer chicken, cut up
3 tablespoons butter *or* margarine
1 cup chopped celery
1 6-ounce can water chestnuts,
   drained and sliced
½ teaspoon dried rosemary
2 cups cooked long grain rice
¾ cup dry white wine
1 16-ounce can apricot halves
4 teaspoons cornstarch

In skillet brown the chicken in butter. Season with salt and pepper; remove and set aside. In same skillet add celery, water chestnuts, rosemary, and ¼ teaspoon salt; cook till celery is tender. Remove from heat. Add rice and ½ *cup* of the wine. Turn into 12x7½x2-inch baking dish; top with chicken. Cover; bake at 375° for 1 hour. Drain apricots, reserving syrup. Combine syrup, cornstarch, and ¼ teaspoon salt; cook till thickened. Add remaining wine. Arrange apricots around chicken. Pour glaze over all. Bake, uncovered, 10 minutes more. Makes 4 servings.

Calypso Java Bread

Baked in coffee cans for gift-size loaves—

- **3 cups packaged biscuit mix**
- **¾ cup packed brown sugar**
- **¼ cup all-purpose flour**
- **1 tablespoon instant coffee crystals**
- **½ cup milk**
- **1 cup mashed ripe banana (2 bananas)**
- **1 beaten egg**
- **1 cup snipped pitted dates**
- **½ cup chopped walnuts**

In mixing bowl combine biscuit mix, brown sugar, and flour. Dissolve coffee crystals in milk; add all at once to dry ingredients along with banana and egg. Stir just till blended. Stir in dates and nuts. Grease bottoms of two 1-pound coffee cans. Divide batter between cans. Bake at 350° for 50 minutes; cool 10 minutes. Loosen sides of loaves with spatula; remove from cans. Makes 2 loaves.

Pimiento Cheese Rolls

- **2 cups all-purpose flour**
- **1 package active dry yeast**

• • •

- **⅔ cup water**
- **½ cup cheese spread with pimiento**
- **¼ cup shortening**
- **2 tablespoons sugar**
- **1 teaspoon salt**
- **1 egg**
- **Poppy seed**

In large mixing bowl combine *1 cup* of the flour and the yeast. In a saucepan combine water, cheese spread, shortening, sugar, and salt. Heat and stir just till warm (115° to 120°)—all of shortening may not be melted. Stir into dry mixture in mixing bowl; add egg. Beat at low speed of electric mixer for ½ minute, scraping sides of bowl. Beat 3 minutes at high speed. By hand, stir in remaining 1 cup flour. Cover and let dough rest 10 minutes. Spoon dough into 12 well-greased 2½-inch muffin pans. Sprinkle poppy seed atop. Let rise in warm place till almost double (1 to 1¼ hours). Bake at 350° for 15 to 18 minutes. Remove from pan; cool. Makes 12 rolls.

Cottage Cheese Buns

Biscuit-like bun shown on pages 38 and 39—

- **3 cups all-purpose flour**
- **2 tablespoons sugar**
- **1 package active dry yeast**
- **1 12-ounce carton cream-style cottage cheese (1½ cups)**
- **½ cup butter *or* margarine**
- **1 egg**

In large mixing bowl combine *1 cup* of the flour, sugar, yeast, and ¾ teaspoon salt. Heat and stir cottage cheese, butter, and ¼ cup water just till warm (115° to 120°)—all of butter may not be melted. Add to dry mixture; add egg. Beat at low speed of electric mixer for ½ minute, scraping sides of bowl. Beat 3 minutes at high speed. By hand, stir in remaining flour. Turn onto lightly floured surface. Cover; let rest 10 minutes. Shape into 16 rolls; place 2 to 3 inches apart on greased baking sheet. Cover; let rise in warm place till double (30 to 45 minutes). Bake at 350° for 15 to 18 minutes. Makes 16 rolls.

Corn-Bacon Bake

Cook 4 slices bacon till crisp; drain, reserving 3 tablespoons drippings. Crumble bacon finely; set aside. Stir together 1 cup all-purpose flour, ½ cup sugar, 1 teaspoon baking soda, and 1 teaspoon salt. Stir in 2 cups white cornmeal. Stir in 2 cups buttermilk, reserved drippings, and bacon; mix well. Pour into well-greased 1½-quart casserole. Bake at 350° till top is golden brown, 60 to 70 minutes. Cool. Invert; cut into thin slices. Makes 1 loaf.

Irish Soda Bread

Stir together 3 cups all-purpose flour, 2 tablespoons packed brown sugar, 2 teaspoons baking powder, 1 teaspoon baking soda, and 1 teaspoon salt. Stir in ½ cup dried currants and 1 teaspoon caraway seed. Add 1½ cups buttermilk *or* sour milk; stir till moistened. Turn into greased 8x1½-inch round baking pan. Bake at 350° till browned, about 40 minutes. Cool 10 minutes; remove. Cool. Makes 1.

Marble Muffins

Bring on the coffee with these spicy gems —

¾ cup granulated sugar
½ cup shortening
1 egg
2 cups all-purpose flour
2 teaspoons baking powder
½ teaspoon salt
¾ cup milk

• • •

2 tablespoons light molasses
½ teaspoon ground cinnamon
½ teaspoon ground nutmeg
⅛ teaspoon ground cloves
¼ cup packed brown sugar
2 tablespoons chopped walnuts
1 tablespoon all-purpose flour
1 tablespoon butter *or* margarine,
    melted
½ teaspoon ground cinnamon

Cream together granulated sugar and shortening. Add egg, beating well. Stir together the 2 cups flour, the baking powder, and salt. Add to creamed mixture alternately with milk, beating after each addition. Divide batter in half. To one half, add molasses, ½ teaspoon cinnamon, the nutmeg, and cloves; mix well. Spoon batters alternately into greased 2½-inch muffin pans. Combine remaining ingredients; mix well and spoon atop batter. Bake at 350° for 25 to 30 minutes. Makes 16 muffins.

Corn Spoon Bread

2 beaten eggs
1 8½-ounce package corn muffin mix
1 8-ounce can cream-style corn
1 8-ounce can whole kernel corn,
    drained
1 cup dairy sour cream
½ cup butter *or* margarine, melted
1 cup shredded Swiss cheese
    (4 ounces)

Combine first 6 ingredients. Spread in 11x7½x1½-inch baking pan. Bake at 350° for 35 minutes. Sprinkle cheese atop; bake till knife comes out clean, 10 to 15 minutes longer. Makes 8 servings.

Stagger baking pans

To ensure an even distribution of heat and overall airflow when baking, allow at least 2 inches of space all around each pan in the oven. When the baking pans need two oven racks, remember to arrange them so that the baking pans on the top rack are not directly over the pans on the bottom rack.

Horseradish Dinner Rolls

1 13¾-ounce package hot roll mix
½ cup warm water (110°)
1 egg
½ cup cream-style cottage cheese
1 tablespoon prepared horseradish
2 teaspoons sugar
1 teaspoon salt

• • •

1 tablespoon butter *or* margarine,
    melted
1 teaspoon prepared horseradish

In large bowl soften yeast from hot roll mix in the warm water. Stir in egg, cottage cheese, the 1 tablespoon horseradish, sugar, and salt. Add flour mixture from hot roll mix; blend well. Cover and let rise till almost double (about 45 minutes). Punch down. Shape into 32 balls; place two balls in each of 16 greased 2½-inch muffin cups. Combine butter and 1 teaspoon horseradish; brush over dough. Cover; let rise till double (about 30 minutes). Bake at 375° till golden brown, 15 to 20 minutes. Makes 16 rolls.

Toasted French Slices

4 1-inch slices French bread
3 tablespoons butter, softened
1 tablespoon grated Parmesan cheese

Spread French bread with softened butter on both sides. Arrange slices in a single layer in a 12x7½x2-inch baking dish. Sprinkle with Parmesan cheese. Bake at 350° till golden brown, about 15 minutes. Makes 2 servings.

Brussels Sprouts Bake

2 10-ounce packages frozen Brussels
    sprouts
2 beaten eggs
1½ cups soft bread crumbs (2 slices
    bread)
1 10¾-ounce can condensed cream of
    mushroom soup
½ cup shredded sharp American
    cheese (2 ounces)
2 tablespoons chopped onion
    Dash pepper
1 tablespoon butter *or* margarine,
    melted

Cook Brussels sprouts, following package directions; cut into quarters. In bowl combine eggs, ½ *cup* of the crumbs, soup, cheese, onion, and pepper. Stir in sprouts. Turn into a 1½-quart casserole. Combine remaining crumbs and melted butter; sprinkle atop sprouts. Bake, uncovered, at 350° for 50 to 55 minutes. Serves 6 to 8.

Spinach-Stuffed Onions

1 10-ounce package frozen chopped
    spinach
1 3-ounce package cream cheese,
    softened
1 egg
½ cup soft bread crumbs (about ½
    slice bread)
¼ cup grated Parmesan cheese
¼ cup milk
¼ teaspoon salt
1 large flat white onion

Cook spinach according to package directions; drain well and set aside. Beat together cream cheese and egg till fluffy. Add bread crumbs, Parmesan, milk, salt, and dash pepper; mix well. Stir in spinach. Peel onion; cut in half crosswise. Separate layers to form shells; place shells in 9x9x2-inch baking dish. Fill base of shells with any remaining small onion pieces. Spoon spinach mixture into shells. Cover dish with foil. Bake at 350° till onion shells are tender and filling is set, 35 to 40 minutes. Makes 6 servings.

Hot Bean Trio

8 slices bacon
⅔ cup sugar
2 tablespoons cornstarch
1 teaspoon salt
1 teaspoon chili powder
    Several dashes bottled hot pepper
    sauce
    Dash pepper
¾ cup vinegar
½ cup water
2 16-ounce cans cut green beans
2 16-ounce cans red kidney beans
1 15-ounce can garbanzo beans

In large skillet cook bacon till crisp; drain, reserving ¼ cup drippings. Crumble bacon and set aside. In same skillet combine reserved drippings, sugar, cornstarch, salt, chili powder, hot pepper sauce, and pepper. Stir in vinegar and water; cook and stir till thickened and bubbly. Drain all the beans; rinse the kidney beans. Add vinegar mixture to the beans with *about half* the crumbled bacon; stir to coat beans. Turn into 2-quart casserole. Bake, uncovered, at 350° till heated through, about 30 minutes. Sprinkle remaining bacon atop. Makes 12 servings.

Broccoli Supreme

1 beaten egg
1 10-ounce package frozen chopped
    broccoli, partially thawed
1 8-ounce can cream-style corn
1 tablespoon grated onion
¼ teaspoon salt
    Dash pepper
3 tablespoons butter *or* margarine
1 cup herb-seasoned stuffing mix

In mixing bowl combine egg, broccoli, cream-style corn, onion, salt, and pepper. In small saucepan melt butter or margarine; add herb-seasoned stuffing mix, tossing to coat. Stir ¾ *cup* of the buttered stuffing mix into vegetable mixture. Turn into ungreased 1-quart casserole. Sprinkle with remaining ¼ cup stuffing mix. Bake, uncovered, at 350° for 35 to 40 minutes. Makes 4 to 6 servings.

Cheesy Lima Casserole

1 cup large dry lima beans (8 ounces)
½ cup shredded American cheese
(2 ounces)
⅓ cup chopped onion
½ teaspoon salt
¼ teaspoon rubbed sage
Dash pepper
• • •
3 slices bacon, crisp-cooked, drained,
and crumbled

Rinse lima beans; place in large saucepan with 2½ cups water. Soak overnight. (Or, bring to boiling. Cover and simmer 2 minutes; remove from heat. Let stand 1 hour.) Do not drain. Simmer, covered, for 1 hour. Stir in the shredded cheese, onion, salt, sage, and pepper; mix well. Turn mixture into a 1-quart casserole. Top with cooked bacon. Bake, uncovered, at 350° about 35 minutes. Top with additional triangles of cheese, if desired. Makes 3 or 4 servings.

Grated Potato Casserole

3 medium potatoes, peeled
and cubed (3 cups)
1 cup milk
3 eggs
1 cup cubed sharp American
cheese (4 ounces)
½ small onion, cut in pieces
3 tablespoons all-purpose flour
2 tablespoons margarine *or* butter,
softened
½ teaspoon salt
⅛ teaspoon pepper

Place *half* of the cubed potatoes in blender container; add cold water to cover. Blend just till all potatoes are coarsely chopped. *Do not overblend.* Drain well and set aside. Repeat with remaining potatoes. Combine milk, eggs, cheese, onion, flour, margarine, salt, and pepper in blender container; cover and blend till combined. In large bowl combine potatoes and cheese mixture. Pour into greased 10x6x2-inch baking dish. Bake, uncovered, at 350° till done, 45 to 50 minutes. Makes 6 servings.

Onion-Stuffed Acorn Squash

A perfect vegetable accompaniment for ham —

2 medium acorn squash
1 10-ounce package frozen tiny onions
in cream sauce
1 cup shredded sharp
American cheese (4 ounces)
• • •
Salt
1 cup soft bread crumbs (1½ slices
bread)
2 tablespoons snipped parsley
2 tablespoons butter *or* margarine,
melted

Cut squash in half lengthwise; remove seeds. Place squash, cut side down, in shallow baking pan. Bake at 350° for 35 to 40 minutes. Meanwhile, cook onions according to package directions; stir in cheese till melted. Turn squash cut side up; sprinkle with a little salt. Spoon in onion mixture. Combine crumbs and snipped parsley; toss with melted butter or margarine. Sprinkle atop onions. Bake 15 to 20 minutes longer. Makes 4 servings.

Profit from oven cooking

Save time in the kitchen and hold the line on the utility bill by baking extra foods along with oven meals. The recipes below are good examples of bake-along foods because you do not serve them hot from the oven. You cook them with one oven meal, chill, and serve them later.

Oven-Cooked Applesauce: Place 8 medium apples, peeled, cored, and sliced (8 cups); 1 cup water; ½ cup sugar; and ⅛ teaspoon ground cinnamon in a 2-quart casserole or 12x7½x2-inch baking dish. Cover and bake at 350° till apples are tender, 50 minutes. Uncover, stir gently; chill till ready to serve. Makes 4 cups.

Oven-Cooked Cranberries: In a 13x9x2-inch baking pan stir together 1 pound cranberries (about 4 cups), 2 cups sugar, and ¼ cup water. Cover pan. Bake at 350°, stirring occasionally till skins of berries pop, 50 to 60 minutes. Chill. Makes 4 cups.

Texas Bean Barbecue

8 slices bacon, chopped
1 cup chopped onion
2 20-ounce cans yellow hominy, drained
2 16-ounce cans red kidney beans, drained
1 15-ounce can tomato sauce
¼ cup chopped canned green chili peppers
2 tablespoons vinegar
2 teaspoons Worcestershire sauce
2 teaspoons prepared mustard
1 teaspoon salt

Cook bacon till almost crisp; drain, reserving 2 tablespoons drippings. Cook onion in reserved drippings till tender but not brown. Combine onion and bacon with remaining ingredients. Turn into 2-quart casserole. Bake, covered, at 350° for 1½ hours. Serves 10.

Potatoes Romanoff

1 8-ounce container Neufchâtel cheese dip with bacon and horseradish (1 cup)
1 cup cream-style cottage cheese
½ cup shredded sharp American cheese (2 ounces)
2 tablespoons snipped parsley
6 cups cubed cooked potatoes
Paprika

Combine bacon-horseradish dip, cottage cheese, *half* the shredded American cheese, the parsley, and 1 teaspoon salt. Add potatoes; toss gently to coat. Turn potato mixture into 10x6x2-inch baking dish. Sprinkle with paprika. Bake, uncovered, at 350° till heated through, 30 to 35 minutes. Top with remaining shredded cheese; bake till cheese melts, 3 to 4 minutes more. Makes 8 servings.

◀ **Looking for an out-of-the-ordinary** vegetable dish? Choose from *Texas Bean Barbecue,* *Gilded Acorn Squash,* or *Potatoes Romanoff.* Any of these vegetables tastily completes an oven meal baked at a moderate temperature.

Vera Cruz Tomatoes

This dish is shown on pages 38 and 39—

3 slices bacon
¼ cup chopped onion
8 ounces fresh spinach, snipped
½ cup dairy sour cream
Dash bottled hot pepper sauce
4 medium tomatoes
½ cup shredded mozzarella cheese (2 ounces)

Cook bacon till crisp; drain, reserving 2 tablespoons drippings. Crumble bacon; set aside. Cook onion in reserved drippings till tender; stir in spinach. Cook, covered, till tender, 3 to 5 minutes. Remove from heat; stir in sour cream, bacon, and hot pepper sauce. Cut tops from tomatoes; remove centers, leaving shells. Drain. Salt shells; place in 8x8x2-inch baking pan. Fill with spinach mixture. Bake at 375° for 20 to 25 minutes. Top with cheese; bake till cheese melts, 2 to 3 minutes more. Makes 4 servings.

Gilded Acorn Squash

Fresh oranges make squash a winter sensation—

2 acorn squash, halved and seeds removed
2 oranges
2 tablespoons packed brown sugar
2 tablespoons butter *or* margarine, melted
Dash ground cloves
2 tablespoons chopped pecans

Cut a thin slice off bottom of each squash so it will sit flat in the pan. Place, cut side down, in shallow baking pan. Bake at 350° till almost tender, but not soft, 40 to 45 minutes. Grate 1 teaspoon orange peel; remove remaining peel, then section and seed oranges. Combine grated orange peel, orange sections, brown sugar, butter, cloves, and ½ teaspoon salt. Turn squash cut side up. Scoop out squash, leaving ½-inch shell. Combine squash and fruit mixture; spoon into hollows. Bake, uncovered, at 350° till heated through, about 15 minutes longer. Garnish with the chopped pecans. Makes 4 servings.

Cheddar-Topped Baked Apples

  6 large baking apples
  ¾ cup raisins
  1 tablespoon butter *or* margarine
  1 cup sugar
  1 cup water
      • • •
  ½ cup shredded Cheddar cheese
      (2 ounces)
  1 tablespoon milk
  1 3-ounce package cream cheese,
      softened

Core apples and peel strip from top of each. Place apples in 13x9x2-inch baking dish. Into center of each apple, spoon *2 tablespoons* of the raisins and ½ *teaspoon* of the butter or margarine. In saucepan combine sugar and water; bring to boiling. Pour hot sugar syrup over apples. Bake, uncovered, at 350° about 1 hour, basting occasionally with syrup.

Have Cheddar cheese at room temperature. Beat milk into softened cream cheese till fluffy. Stir in Cheddar cheese till mixture is blended. To serve, top apples with cheese mixture. Makes 6 servings.

Fresh Fruit Crisp

Enjoy this dessert year-round, choosing your favorite fruit of each season —

  ½ cup quick-cooking rolled oats
  ½ cup packed brown sugar
  ¼ cup all-purpose flour
  ½ teaspoon ground cinnamon
      Dash salt
  ¼ cup butter *or* margarine
      • • •
  5 cups sliced, peeled peaches, apples,
      or pears
      Vanilla ice cream *or* light cream

Mix together the oats, brown sugar, flour, cinnamon, and salt; cut in butter or margarine till mixture is crumbly. Set aside. Place the fruit in a 10x6x2-inch baking dish. Sprinkle the oat mixture over fruit. Bake at 350° till fruit is tender, about 40 minutes. Serve the fruit crisp warm with ice cream or light cream. Makes 6 servings.

Apple-Date Dream

  2 cups all-purpose flour
  1 cup sugar
  1½ teaspoons baking soda
  1 teaspoon salt
  1 teaspoon ground cinnamon
  ½ teaspoon ground allspice
      • • •
  2 beaten eggs
  1 21-ounce can apple pie filling
  ½ cup cooking oil
  1 teaspoon vanilla
  1 cup chopped pitted dates
  ¼ cup chopped walnuts

Stir together thoroughly the flour, sugar, baking soda, salt, cinnamon, and allspice. Combine eggs, pie filling, oil, and vanilla; stir into flour mixture and mix well. Stir in dates and nuts. Pour into greased and floured 13x9x2-inch baking dish. Bake at 350° for 40 to 45 minutes. Cool. Cut in squares. Serve with a dollop of whipped cream, if desired. Serves 12.

Banana Bread Pudding

COST-CUTTING RECIPE

  4 slices day-old bread
  ¼ cup margarine, softened
  1 cup apricot nectar
  2 beaten egg yolks
  ½ cup sugar
  2 medium bananas, sliced (about 1½
      cups)
  2 egg whites
  ½ teaspoon vanilla
  ¼ teaspoon cream of tartar

Spread bread on both sides with softened margarine; cut into ½-inch cubes. Combine nectar, egg yolks, and ¼ *cup* of the sugar; add bread, stirring till moistened. Turn *half* of the mixture into 1½-quart casserole. Top with banana slices; cover with remaining bread mixture. Bake at 350° for 35 minutes. Beat egg whites, vanilla, and cream of tartar to soft peaks. Gradually add the remaining ¼ cup sugar, beating till stiff peaks form. Spread egg white mixture over hot pudding, sealing to edge of casserole. Bake 12 to 15 minutes more. Makes 6 servings.

Peanut Butter Pudding Cake

1 cup all-purpose flour
1¼ cups packed brown sugar
2 teaspoons baking powder
½ cup milk
⅓ cup chunk-style peanut butter
2 tablespoons cooking oil
1 teaspoon vanilla
1½ cups hot water
   Vanilla ice cream

In a bowl stir together the flour, ¾ *cup* of the brown sugar, baking powder, and ½ teaspoon salt. Stir in milk, peanut butter, cooking oil, and vanilla. Spread in greased 8x8x2-inch baking dish. Sprinkle with remaining brown sugar. Carefully pour hot water over surface. Bake at 350° for 45 minutes. Serve warm with ice cream. Makes 9 servings.

Mocha Rice Soufflé

2 cups milk
¼ cup long grain rice
½ teaspoon salt
⅓ cup sugar
3 tablespoons chopped almonds, toasted
2 tablespoons butter *or* margarine
2 1-ounce squares unsweetened chocolate, melted
1 tablespoon instant coffee crystals
1 teaspoon vanilla
3 egg whites
3 tablespoons sugar
4 marshmallows

In saucepan combine milk, rice, and salt. Bring just to boiling; reduce heat and cook, covered, till rice is tender, about 20 minutes. Remove from heat; stir in ⅓ cup sugar, almonds, butter, chocolate, coffee crystals, and vanilla. Beat egg whites till soft peaks form; gradually add the 3 tablespoons sugar, beating to stiff peaks. Fold chocolate mixture into egg whites. Turn into four 8-ounce soufflé dishes. Bake at 350° till knife inserted just off-center comes out clean, 20 minutes. Top each with a marshmallow; bake 5 to 8 minutes more. Makes 4 servings.

Cherry Cottage Pudding

In a bowl combine 1½ cups pitted fresh tart red cherries, chopped, and ½ cup granulated sugar. Let stand about 10 minutes; drain, reserving the liquid for sauce. Cream together 6 tablespoons butter, ⅓ cup granulated sugar, and ¼ cup packed brown sugar. Add 1 egg; beat well. Thoroughly stir together 1¾ cups all-purpose flour, 2½ teaspoons baking powder, and ½ teaspoon salt. Add to the creamed mixture alternately with ⅔ cup milk, beating well. Fold in the drained cherries. Turn into a greased and floured 9x9x2-inch baking pan. Bake at 350° till cake tests done, about 35 minutes. Serve with Cherry Sauce. Serves 9.

Cherry Sauce: In saucepan combine 2 tablespoons cornstarch, 2 tablespoons granulated sugar, and dash salt. Add enough water to the reserved cherry syrup from the dessert to make 1¼ cups liquid. Add to cornstarch mixture along with 1 cup pitted fresh tart red cherries. Cook and stir till thickened and bubbly. Stir in a few drops almond extract and 4 drops red food coloring. Cool slightly. Serve the warm sauce over dessert.

Green Grape Bake

This subtly spiced dessert resembles a crisp—

4 cups seedless *or* seeded green grapes
1 tablespoon lemon juice
⅛ teaspoon ground cinnamon
⅛ teaspoon ground nutmeg
• • •
½ cup all-purpose flour
½ cup packed brown sugar
¼ cup butter *or* margarine
• • •
   Vanilla ice cream

Place the grapes in a 1-quart casserole. Sprinkle with the lemon juice, cinnamon, and nutmeg. In a bowl combine the flour and brown sugar. Cut in the butter or margarine till the mixture is crumbly. Stir *half* of the crumb mixture into the grapes. Sprinkle remaining crumb mixture over the top. Bake at 375° for 40 minutes. Serve the dessert warm or cold topped with a scoop of vanilla ice cream. Serves 6.

Pineapple Upside-Down Cakes

1 8¼-ounce can pineapple tidbits
3 tablespoons butter *or* margarine
½ cup packed brown sugar
4 maraschino cherries, halved
1 package 1-layer-size yellow cake
   mix

Drain pineapple; reserve syrup. Melt butter; stir in *1 tablespoon* reserved syrup. Place about ½ *tablespoon* butter mixture in each of eight 6-ounce custard cups. Add *1 tablespoon* brown sugar to each. Arrange pineapple atop sugar. Place cherry half in center. Prepare cake mix, following package directions and using remaining pineapple syrup plus enough water to equal liquid called for on package. Spoon about ¼ *cup* batter into each cup. Bake at 350° for 25 to 30 minutes. Let stand 5 minutes; invert onto plate. Makes 8 servings.

Curried Three-Fruit Compote

1 13¼-ounce can pineapple chunks
1 11-ounce package dried apricots
   (3 cups)
1½ cups seedless green grapes
½ cup packed brown sugar
1 to 2 teaspoons curry powder
2 7-ounce bottles ginger ale
   (about 2 cups)
   Brown sugar
   Dairy sour cream

In 2-quart casserole combine the *undrained* pineapple, apricots, and grapes. Stir together brown sugar and curry powder; sprinkle over fruit. Pour in ginger ale. Cover and bake at 350° for 45 to 60 minutes, stirring once or twice. Serve warm or chilled sprinkled with brown sugar and topped with a dollop of dairy sour cream. Makes 12 servings.

For generations, many Americans have enjoyed *Pineapple Upside-Down Cakes.* Our version of this taste-tempting dessert is prepared in miniature form for individual servings. Be sure to include this classic recipe in your collection of family favorites.

Date-Orange Pudding Cake

In saucepan combine ½ cup packed brown sugar and 1 tablespoon cornstarch. Stir in ¾ cup water; cook and stir till mixture thickens and bubbles. Remove from heat; stir in ½ cup snipped pitted dates. Cool. Stir in one 11-ounce can mandarin orange sections, drained. Turn fruit mixture into well-greased 10-inch fluted tube pan.

In large bowl stir together 1½ cups all-purpose flour, 2 teaspoons baking soda, 1 teaspoon salt, ½ teaspoon ground cinnamon, ½ teaspoon ground ginger, and ¼ teaspoon ground cloves. Add 1½ cups fine dry bread crumbs, 1½ cups orange marmalade, 1 cup milk, and ½ cup cooking oil; mix well. Stir in 1 cup snipped pitted dates. Gently spoon batter over fruit in pan. Bake at 350° till cake tests done, about 50 minutes. Cool 10 minutes; invert onto serving plate. Serve warm or cool. Makes 12 to 16 servings.

Peach-Berry Shortcake

Fresh peaches and blueberries make this company-size gingerbread a dessert extravaganza—

    1 14-ounce package gingerbread mix
    ½ cup packed brown sugar
    2 tablespoons cornstarch
    1 cup water
    2 cups fresh blueberries
    2 cups sliced fresh peaches
    2 tablespoons butter *or* margarine
    2 tablespoons lemon juice
        • • •
        Frozen whipped dessert topping, thawed

Prepare the gingerbread mix according to package directions, *except bake in a 13x9x2-inch baking pan* at 350° till done, about 20 minutes. In a saucepan combine the brown sugar and cornstarch; gradually blend in water. Stir in blueberries. Cook and stir over medium heat till the mixture is thickened and bubbly. Stir in the sliced peaches, butter or margarine, and lemon juice. Spoon the hot fruit sauce over squares of warm gingerbread. Serve with a dollop of whipped dessert topping. Makes about 12 servings.

Mince Cottage Pudding

    ½ cup boiling water
    ½ cup finely snipped pitted dates
    ½ cup butter *or* margarine
    ½ cup packed brown sugar
    2 eggs
    2 cups prepared mincemeat
        • • •
  2¼ cups all-purpose flour
    1 tablespoon baking powder
    1 teaspoon salt
    ¼ teaspoon ground nutmeg
    ¼ cup chopped nuts
      Vanilla Sauce

In bowl pour boiling water over dates; cool. Cream together the butter and brown sugar till light. Add eggs, one at a time, beating well after each. Stir mincemeat and date mixture into creamed mixture. Stir together the flour, baking powder, salt, and nutmeg; mix with creamed mixture just till blended. Stir in chopped nuts. Pour mixture into a greased and floured 13x9x2-inch baking dish. Bake at 350° till done, 35 to 40 minutes. Cut into squares. Serve warm with Vanilla Sauce. Makes 12 servings.

Vanilla Sauce: In a bowl beat 3 egg yolks with ¾ cup sifted powdered sugar, 1 teaspoon vanilla, and dash salt till thick and lemon-colored. Whip 1 cup whipping cream; fold whipped cream into sauce. Chill. Stir sauce before serving.

Speedy Mincemeat Squares

Drain one 17-ounce can fruit cocktail, reserving ½ cup syrup. In bowl combine drained fruit, one 9-ounce package condensed mincemeat, and reserved syrup; mix well to soften mincemeat. Combine 2½ cups packaged biscuit mix, 1 cup sugar, 3 tablespoons melted butter *or* margarine, and 1 egg; mix till crumbly. Press *half* the crumb mixture into greased 13x9x2-inch baking pan. Spread fruit mixture atop; cover with remaining crumb mixture, pressing in lightly. Bake at 375° for 30 to 35 minutes. Cut into squares; top with a scoop of vanilla ice cream. Sprinkle with toasted coconut, if desired. Makes 12 servings.

Hot oven dishes

Sometimes you can speed up a meal by using a hot oven (400° to 450° F.) In this section are recipes for main dishes, vegetables, breads, and desserts that you can bake together in a hot temperature oven.

Corn Bread-Topped Chicken Pie

Good hot dish for a cold day—

1 52-ounce can whole chicken
½ cup yellow cornmeal
½ cup all-purpose flour
1 tablespoon sugar
2 teaspoons baking powder
¼ teaspoon salt
½ cup milk
1 beaten egg
2 tablespoons cooking oil
⅓ cup chopped onion
⅓ cup chopped green pepper
2 tablespoons margarine *or* butter
1 10¾-ounce can condensed cream of
   mushroom soup
¼ cup all-purpose flour
1 teaspoon ground sage
1 10-ounce package frozen mixed
   vegetables, cooked and drained
1 3-ounce can chopped mushrooms,
   drained

Drain chicken; reserve 1 cup broth. Remove chicken from bones; cube chicken and set aside. To make corn bread, in bowl stir together the cornmeal, the ½ cup flour, sugar, baking powder, and salt. Add milk, beaten egg, and oil. Beat with electric mixer or rotary beater just till smooth; set aside. In large saucepan cook onion and green pepper in margarine till tender. Stir together soup, ¼ cup flour, and sage. Stir soup mixture into cooked onion and green pepper. Add reserved chicken broth, cooked mixed vegetables, and mushrooms. Cook and stir till thickened and bubbly. Stir in chicken; return mixture to boiling. Pour bubbling chicken mixture into 2-quart casserole. Spoon corn bread batter atop casserole. Bake at 425° till corn bread is done, 18 to 20 minutes. Makes 6 servings.

Oven-Baked Chicken Kiev

1 cup butter *or* margarine
2 tablespoons snipped chives
¾ teaspoon grated lemon peel
1 tablespoon lemon juice
¼ teaspoon freshly ground black pepper
6 large whole chicken breasts, skinned
   and boned (about 3 pounds)
1 beaten egg
  All-purpose flour
⅔ cup fine dry bread crumbs

Cream butter till fluffy. Add chives, peel, juice, and pepper; mix. Shape ¾ *cup* mixture into six 2-inch sticks. Freeze firm. Place chicken between sheets of waxed paper; pound to flatten. Salt. Place 1 butter stick on each. Roll up; secure with wooden picks. Combine egg and 1 tablespoon water. Coat chicken with flour. Dip in egg; coat with crumbs. In skillet heat remaining butter mixture. Add chicken; cook over medium heat 10 to 15 minutes, turning to cook all sides. Bake in shallow baking pan at 400° for 20 minutes. Serve over hot cooked noodles, if desired. Makes 6 servings.

Ham and Apple Turnovers

Unroll pastry from 1 package refrigerated apple turnovers; separate. Roll each section to 5½-inch square. Cut 12 ounces fully cooked ham in small cubes to measure 2 cups. Place ¼ *cup* ham on each pastry section. Mix filling from turnovers with ¼ cup catsup. Place *1 tablespoon* filling mixture over ham in each turnover. Bring corners of pastry together to form triangle; seal. Bake on baking sheet at 400° till brown, 10 to 12 minutes. Heat one 8½-ounce can applesauce and 1 tablespoon catsup; serve hot over turnovers. Makes 8.

Impress guests by serving *Oven-Baked Chicken Kiev*. This buttery chicken dish is made without the bother and mess of deep-fat frying.

The chicken breasts can be browned ahead of time, if desired, then popped into the oven to bake as guests begin to arrive.

Stuffed Baked Franks

Good for a Saturday or anytime you get the family together for a quick lunch—

 1 pound *large* frankfurters (5 or 6)
 ¼ cup finely chopped onion
 1 tablespoon butter *or* margarine
   • • •
 2 cups herb-seasoned stuffing mix
 ¼ cup catsup
 1 tablespoon sweet pickle relish
 3 slices sharp American cheese
  (3 ounces)

Cut franks lengthwise almost to opposite side. Cook onion in butter till tender but not brown. Combine stuffing mix, onion, catsup, pickle relish, and ¾ cup water; mix well. Mound stuffing atop franks. Place on baking sheet. Bake at 400° till heated, 10 to 12 minutes. Cut cheese slices in strips and place atop franks; return to oven and heat till cheese melts, about 3 minutes. Makes 5 or 6 servings.

Chili Supper Casserole

 ½ pound ground beef
 ¼ cup chopped onion
 ¼ cup chopped green pepper
 1 two-can-pack chili dinner with beef
  and beans
 1 8-ounce can whole kernel corn,
  drained
 1 4-ounce package shredded sharp
  Cheddar cheese (1 cup)
 1 8½-ounce package corn muffin mix

Cook ground beef, onion, and pepper till meat is browned and vegetables are tender. Stir in both cans of chili dinner, corn, and cheese; heat till bubbling hot. Pour into 10x6x2-inch baking dish. Prepare muffin mix, following package directions. Spoon *half* the batter in diagonal bands across top of casserole. Spoon remaining batter into 3 or 4 paper bake cup-lined muffin pans. Bake both at 400° for 17 minutes. Makes 8 servings.

Hominy-Sausage Bake

Good with salad for a meal—

1 pound bulk pork sausage
¼ cup chopped onion
1 16-ounce can yellow hominy, drained
1 10¾-ounce can condensed tomato soup
¼ cup milk
¾ cup shredded sharp American cheese
    (3 ounces)
1 package refrigerated biscuits
    (6 biscuits)
2 tablespoons margarine, melted
¼ cup yellow cornmeal

In skillet cook sausage and onion till sausage is browned. Drain off excess fat. Stir hominy, soup, and milk into sausage; bring to boiling. Stir in cheese; heat just to boiling. Turn hot mixture into 1½-quart casserole. Dip biscuits in melted margarine, then in cornmeal. Arrange atop hot mixture in casserole. Bake, uncovered, at 400° till biscuits are golden, about 20 minutes. Makes 4 to 6 servings.

Bacon-Leek Pie

6 slices bacon, cut in 1-inch pieces
6 medium leeks, thinly sliced
    (about 2 cups)
1 tablespoon all-purpose flour
½ teaspoon celery seed
1 cup light cream
2 tablespoons dry sherry
4 slightly beaten eggs
1 unbaked 9-inch pastry shell

Cook bacon till crisp; place on paper toweling and set aside. Drain fat from skillet; reserve ¼ cup drippings. Cook leeks in reserved drippings till tender but not brown; stir occasionally. Stir in flour, celery seed, 1 teaspoon salt, and ¼ teaspoon pepper. Add cream; cook and stir till mixture thickens and bubbles. Stir in sherry. Remove from heat. Stir a moderate amount of hot mixture into beaten eggs; return to hot mixture in skillet. Stir in bacon. Pour into pastry shell; sprinkle lightly with ground nutmeg, if desired. Bake at 400° till knife inserted just off-center comes out clean, 15 to 18 minutes. Let stand 5 minutes. Serves 6.

Spinach and Bacon Bake

2 10-ounce packages frozen chopped
    spinach
2 slices bacon
½ cup chopped celery
½ cup chopped onion
1 10¾-ounce can condensed cream of
    mushroom soup
1 3-ounce package cream cheese,
    softened
1 tablespoon butter *or* margarine
½ cup croutons

Cook spinach, following package directions; drain. Cook bacon till crisp; drain and crumble, reserving bacon drippings. Cook celery and onion in drippings till tender but not brown. Stir in the soup and cream cheese; heat till cheese melts. Stir in the spinach and crumbled bacon. Turn into 1½-quart casserole. Melt butter; toss with croutons and sprinkle over spinach mixture. Bake, uncovered, at 400° till heated through, 25 to 30 minutes. Makes 8 servings.

Fish and Swiss Bake

1 pound fresh or frozen sole *or*
    flounder fillets (skins removed)
¼ cup snipped parsley
½ cup shredded Swiss cheese
    (2 ounces)
1 tablespoon butter *or* margarine
1 tablespoon all-purpose flour
½ cup evaporated milk
2 tablespoons dry sherry

Thaw and separate frozen fillets. Cut and piece together to make four 6x2½-inch strips. Sprinkle each strip with salt, *1 tablespoon* parsley, and *1 tablespoon* cheese. Roll up jelly-roll fashion around filling. Place fish rolls in 6½x6½x2-inch baking dish. In saucepan melt butter; blend in flour. Stir in milk and wine. Cook and stir till thickened and bubbly; pour over fillets. Bake, uncovered, at 400° till fish flakes easily when tested with a fork, 20 to 25 minutes. Sprinkle with remaining cheese. Bake till cheese melts, 1 to 2 minutes. Trim with additional parsley. Serves 4.

Tuna-Broccoli Bake

Cook two 10-ounce packages frozen cut broccoli, following package directions; set aside. In saucepan melt ¼ cup butter *or* margarine; blend in ¼ cup all-purpose flour, ¾ teaspoon salt, and ⅛ teaspoon pepper. Add 2 cups milk. Cook and stir till thickened and bubbly. Remove from heat. Stir in ½ cup mayonnaise *or* salad dressing. Carefully stir in cooked broccoli; one 9¼-ounce can tuna, drained and broken into chunks; and 3 hard-cooked eggs, cut into wedges. Turn into 2-quart casserole. Sprinkle with paprika. Bake at 400° till heated through, 20 to 25 minutes. Serves 6.

Tuna with Cheese Swirls

Cheesy biscuit pinwheels are the topping —

>   ¼ **cup chopped onion**
>   ¼ **cup chopped green pepper**
>   3 **tablespoons margarine *or* butter**
>   6 **tablespoons all-purpose flour**
>   1 **10½-ounce can condensed cream of**
>   **chicken soup**
> 1½ **cups milk**
>   1 **9¼-ounce can tuna,**
>   **drained and flaked**
>   1 **tablespoon lemon juice**
>   **Cheese Swirls**

Cook chopped onion and green pepper in margarine or butter till tender but not brown. Blend in flour. Stir in soup and milk. Cook, stirring constantly, till sauce is thickened and bubbly. Stir tuna and lemon juice into sauce. Bring to boiling. Turn into 1½-quart casserole. Top boiling mixture with Cheese Swirls. Bake at 425° till swirls brown, about 25 minutes. Makes 4 to 6 servings.

Cheese Swirls: Stir together 1 cup all-purpose flour, 1½ teaspoons baking powder, and ¼ teaspoon salt. Cut in 3 tablespoons shortening till mixture resembles coarse crumbs. Add ⅓ cup milk; mix just till dough follows fork around bowl. Turn out onto lightly floured surface; knead gently for ½ minute. Roll to 8x8-inch square; sprinkle with ½ cup shredded American cheese. Roll up jelly-roll fashion and cut into 8 slices. Place slices, cut side down, on hot tuna mixture.

Koulibiak

A large salmon turnover that serves six —

>   1 **cup finely chopped onion**
>   1 **cup finely chopped carrot**
>   1 **cup finely chopped celery**
>   3 **tablespoons butter *or* margarine**
>   1 **cup thinly sliced fresh mushrooms**
>   ⅓ **cup dairy sour cream**
>   2 **tablespoons lemon juice**
>   ½ **teaspoon salt**
>   ½ **teaspoon dried dillweed**
>   ¼ **teaspoon pepper**
>   1 **16-ounce can salmon, drained and**
>   **bones and skin removed**
>   1 **10-ounce package frozen patty**
>   **shells, thawed (6 shells)**
>   1 **egg**
>   **Lemon-Green Onion Sauce**

In saucepan cook onion, carrot, and celery in butter till tender but not brown. Add mushrooms; stir in sour cream, lemon juice, salt, dillweed, and pepper. Flake salmon and *gently* stir into vegetable mixture. On lightly floured surface press *three* patty shells together; roll to 10x8-inch rectangle.

Place pastry in 15½x10½x1-inch baking pan. Spoon salmon filling down center of pastry. Press remaining three patty shells together; roll to 10x8-inch rectangle. Adjust top crust over salmon filling. Trim edges; reserve trimmings. If desired, cut decorations from reserved trimmings and arrange over loaf. Moisten edges of dough; seal with tines of fork. Brush loaf with mixture of egg and 1 tablespoon water. Slit top for escape of steam. Bake at 400° till browned, about 30 minutes. Transfer to serving platter. Garnish with curly endive or parsley, if desired. Serve with Lemon-Green Onion Sauce. Makes 6 servings.

Lemon-Green Onion Sauce: In saucepan cook ¼ cup chopped green onion and ¼ teaspoon dried dillweed in 2 tablespoons butter *or* margarine till tender. Blend in 1 tablespoon cornstarch. Add 1½ cups chicken broth all at once. Cook and stir till thickened and bubbly. Add 2 teaspoons lemon juice. Stir a moderate amount of hot mixture into 1 slightly beaten egg yolk; return egg mixture to saucepan. Continue cooking, stirring constantly, till mixture is thickened.

Scones

For a cheesy-flavored scone stir ¾ cup shredded sharp Cheddar cheese into dry ingredients just before adding the milk—

  2 cups all-purpose flour
  4 teaspoons baking powder
  2 teaspoons sugar
  ½ cup shortening
  ⅔ cup milk
    Milk

Thoroughly stir together dry ingredients and ½ teaspoon salt. Cut in shortening till crumbly. Make a well; add ⅔ cup milk all at once. Stir with fork just till dough follows fork around bowl. Knead gently on lightly floured surface 10 to 12 strokes. Halve dough. On greased baking sheet pat each half to 8-inch circle. Cut each almost through in 6 wedges. Brush tops with milk. Bake at 425° for 12 to 15 minutes. Makes 12.

Triple Wheat Biscuits

  1¼ cups all-purpose flour
  ½ cup wheat germ
  ¼ cup whole wheat flour
  1 tablespoon baking powder
  1 teaspoon salt
  ¼ cup shortening
  ¾ cup milk

Thoroughly stir together the all-purpose flour, wheat germ, whole wheat flour, baking powder, and salt. Cut in shortening till mixture is crumbly. Add milk; stir with fork till moistened. Knead on lightly floured surface till smooth, about 20 strokes. Roll to ½-inch thickness; cut with floured 2½-inch biscuit cutter. Place biscuits on ungreased baking sheet. Bake at 450° till golden, 8 to 10 minutes. Makes 9 or 10 biscuits.

◄ **These quick breads** are ideal for hot oven baking. And *Banana Split Muffins, Triple Wheat Biscuits, Horseradish-Cheese Loaf,* and *Scones* make attractive and nutritious accompaniments to breakfast, lunch, and dinner.

Horseradish-Cheese Loaf

  1 unsliced 13-inch loaf French *or* sourdough bread
  ½ cup butter *or* margarine, softened
  1 tablespoon grated fresh horseradish
  ½ teaspoon lemon juice
    Few drops bottled hot pepper sauce
  8 slices sharp American cheese (8 ounces)

Slice bread to but not through bottom crust in ¾-inch-thick slices. In bowl cream together butter, horseradish, lemon juice, hot pepper sauce, dash salt, and dash pepper. Spread lightly on all cut surfaces of bread. Halve cheese slices diagonally. Place triangle of cheese in every cut of bread. Wrap loaf in foil. Bake at 400° till cheese melts, 15 to 20 minutes. Makes 8 to 10 servings.

Banana Split Muffins

Besides being attractive muffins, they're easy to make and have a surprise inside—

  2 cups packaged biscuit mix
  ¼ cup sugar
  2 beaten egg yolks
  ⅔ cup milk
  2 tablespoons butter *or* margarine, melted
  ½ small banana
  12 maraschino cherries, halved
  12 walnut pieces
  2 egg whites
  ⅓ cup sugar
  ½ cup flaked coconut

Combine biscuit mix and ¼ cup sugar. Combine egg yolks, milk, and butter; add all at once to dry ingredients, stirring just to moisten. Divide *half* the batter among twelve 2½-inch greased muffin pans. Cut banana into 12 pieces. Place banana piece, cherry half, and walnut piece on each muffin. Cover with remaining batter. Beat egg whites to soft peaks. Gradually add the ⅓ cup sugar; beat till stiff peaks form. Fold in coconut. Place a large spoonful of egg white mixture on each muffin. Top with remaining cherries. Bake at 400° till golden, 12 to 15 minutes. Makes 12.

Coffeetime Gems

    2 cups all-purpose flour
    ½ cup packed brown sugar
    2 teaspoons baking powder
    ½ teaspoon baking soda
    1 beaten egg
    1 cup dairy sour cream
    ½ cup milk
    ¼ cup butter *or* margarine, melted
    2 teaspoons instant coffee crystals
    1 cup chopped pitted dates

Thoroughly stir together first 4 ingredients and ½ teaspoon salt. Combine egg, sour cream, milk, butter, and coffee crystals; stir to dissolve coffee crystals. Add liquid to dry ingredients all at once; stir to moisten. Fold in dates. Fill greased 2½-inch muffin pans ⅔ full. Bake at 400° till done, 20 to 25 minutes. Makes 12 muffins.

Cottage Cheese Muffins

In mixing bowl cream together 3 tablespoons butter and ⅓ cup sugar; beat in ½ cup cream-style cottage cheese and 1 teaspoon grated lemon peel. Add 1 egg; beat well. Add 1¾ cups packaged biscuit mix and ½ cup milk; stir just to moisten. Fill greased 1¾-inch muffin pans ⅔ full. Bake at 400° till done, about 20 minutes. Makes 20 muffins.

Golden Pumpkin Muffins

    2 cups packaged biscuit mix
    ½ cup sugar
    2 teaspoons pumpkin pie spice
    1 beaten egg
    ¾ cup milk
    ½ cup canned pumpkin
    2 tablespoons cooking oil

Combine biscuit mix, sugar, spice, and ¼ teaspoon salt. Combine egg, milk, pumpkin, and cooking oil. Add *half* the liquid mixture to dry ingredients; blend well. Add remaining liquid; stir just to blend. Fill paper bake cup-lined 2½-inch muffin pans ⅔ full. Bake at 400° for 20 to 22 minutes. Makes 12 muffins.

Oatmeal-Raisin Muffins

    1 cup all-purpose flour
    1 tablespoon baking powder
    ¼ cup shortening
    1 cup quick-cooking rolled oats
    1 egg
    1 cup milk
    ½ cup packed brown sugar
    ½ cup raisins
    ¼ cup granulated sugar
    ¼ teaspoon ground cinnamon

Stir together flour, baking powder, and ½ teaspoon salt; cut in shortening. Add oats. Mix egg, milk, and brown sugar; beat well. Stir into dry ingredients. Stir in raisins. Fill greased 2½-inch muffin pans ⅔ full. Mix last 2 ingredients; sprinkle atop. Bake at 425° for 15 to 20 minutes. Makes 12.

Lemon-Blueberry Muffins

Combine 2 cups packaged biscuit mix, ⅓ cup sugar, 2 tablespoons softened butter, and 1 egg. Combine ⅓ cup lemon juice and ⅓ cup milk; add to biscuit mixture and beat well. Fold in 1 cup frozen whole blueberries, thawed and drained. Fill greased 2½-inch muffin pans ⅔ full. Bake at 400° about 25 minutes. While warm, dip muffin tops in melted butter, then in mixture of 2 tablespoons sugar and 1 tablespoon grated lemon peel. Makes 12.

Whole Wheat Granola Muffins

    1¾ cups all-purpose flour
    1 cup granola with raisins
    ½ cup whole wheat flour
    ½ cup packed brown sugar
    1 tablespoon baking powder
    1 beaten egg
    1 cup milk
    ¼ cup cooking oil

Stir together first 5 ingredients and ¼ teaspoon salt. Mix egg, milk, and oil; add to dry ingredients. Stir to moisten. Fill greased 2½-inch muffin pans ⅔ full. Bake at 400° for 20 to 25 minutes. Makes 12 muffins.

Potato-Tomato Bake

    1 4⅝- *or* 5½-ounce package dry
        scalloped potato mix
    1 8-ounce can tomato sauce
    ¼ cup chopped green pepper
    ½ cup canned French-fried onions

In saucepan blend dry sauce mix from potato mix with tomato sauce; add green pepper and 2¼ cups water. Heat to boiling. Add potatoes; mix well. Turn into 1½-quart casserole. Bake, uncovered, at 400° till potatoes are tender, 30 minutes. Top with onions; bake till onions are heated through, about 3 minutes. Serves 4.

Cheese-Sauced Baked Potatoes

    1 cup shredded sharp American cheese
    ½ cup dairy sour cream
    ¼ cup butter *or* margarine, softened
    2 tablespoons chopped green onion
    6 baking potatoes

Have first 4 ingredients at room temperature. Bake potatoes at 425° till done, 45 to 60 minutes. Meanwhile, in small bowl combine cheese, sour cream, butter, and onion; beat till fluffy. To serve, roll potatoes gently under hand. Immediately criss-cross tops with fork; press ends, pushing up to fluff. Top with cheese sauce. Makes 6 servings.

Deviled Stuffed Potatoes

    4 large baking potatoes
    ¼ cup butter *or* margarine, softened
    ½ teaspoon prepared mustard
    ⅛ teaspoon paprika
        Hot milk (about ½ cup)
    1 4½-ounce can deviled ham

Bake potatoes at 425° till done, 45 to 60 minutes. Cut slice from top of each. Reserving shells, scoop out inside; mash. Add butter, mustard, paprika, and ½ teaspoon salt. Beat in enough milk to make stiff consistency. Swirl ham through potatoes. Pile mixture into potato shells; return to oven. Bake till lightly browned, about 20 minutes. Serves 4.

Classic Rice

An oven rice cooked in broth and flavored with onion, Parmesan cheese, and parsley—

    ¼ cup butter *or* margarine
    1 cup long grain rice
    ¼ cup chopped green onions
    1 13¾-ounce can chicken broth
    ¼ cup grated Parmesan cheese
    2 tablespoons snipped parsley
    ½ teaspoon salt
        Dash pepper

In medium skillet melt butter over medium-low heat. Add rice and chopped onions. Cook and stir till each grain of rice is coated and light golden brown. Remove from heat. Add water to chicken broth to make 2 cups. Add broth, cheese, parsley, salt, and pepper to rice. Turn into 1-quart casserole. Bake, covered, at 400° till rice is done, about 45 minutes; stir once about halfway through cooking time. Makes 4 servings.

Corn-Mushroom Bake

A delicious vegetable mixture to serve guests—

    ¼ cup all-purpose flour
    1 16-ounce can cream-style corn
    1 3-ounce package cream cheese,
        cut in cubes
    ½ teaspoon onion salt
    1 16-ounce can whole kernel corn,
        drained
    1 6-ounce can sliced mushrooms,
        drained
    ½ cup shredded Swiss cheese
        (2 ounces)
    1½ cups soft bread crumbs (about
        2½ slices)
    3 tablespoons butter, melted

Thoroughly blend flour into cream-style corn. Add cream cheese and onion salt; heat, stirring constantly, till cheese melts. Stir whole kernel corn, mushrooms, and Swiss cheese into hot mixture. Pour into 1½-quart casserole. Bake, uncovered, at 400° for 20 minutes. Meanwhile, toss crumbs with melted butter. Top casserole with crumbs; bake 10 minutes more. Makes 6 to 8 servings.

Cauli-Broccoli Casserole

In saucepan bring ½ cup water to boiling. Add one 10-ounce package frozen cut broccoli and one 10-ounce package frozen cauliflower; cover. Reduce heat; simmer till vegetables are tender, 12 to 15 minutes. Drain thoroughly. Drain one 4-ounce can chopped mushrooms and toss with vegetables in a 10x6x2-inch baking dish. In saucepan combine one 10¾-ounce can condensed cream of mushroom soup, ¾ cup shredded sharp American cheese, ⅓ cup dry white wine, and 1 teaspoon Worcestershire sauce. Stir over low heat till cheese melts. Pour sauce over vegetables. Melt 2 tablespoons butter; mix with 1½ cups soft bread crumbs. Sprinkle atop casserole. Bake at 400° till hot, about 20 minutes. Serves 6 to 8.

Creamy Swiss Green Beans

¼ cup chopped onion
¼ cup butter *or* margarine
2 tablespoons all-purpose flour
½ cup milk
2 16-ounce cans cut green beans
1 cup dairy sour cream
½ cup shredded Swiss cheese (2 ounces)
1 cup soft bread crumbs

Cook onion in *2 tablespoons* of the butter till tender. Stir in flour, ½ teaspoon salt, and ⅛ teaspoon pepper; add milk. Cook and stir till mixture thickens and bubbles. Drain beans; stir into sauce with sour cream and cheese. Turn into a 10x6x2-inch baking dish. Melt remaining butter; mix with crumbs. Sprinkle over bean mixture. Bake, uncovered, at 400° for 20 to 25 minutes. Makes 6 to 8 servings.

Ginger-Baked Carrots

Quarter 6 medium carrots by slicing in half crosswise and then lengthwise; arrange in 3-cup baking dish. Mix 2 tablespoons packed brown sugar, 2 tablespoons melted butter *or* margarine, 2 teaspoons finely chopped candied ginger, and ¼ teaspoon salt; pour over carrots. Bake, covered, at 400° till carrots are tender, about 1 hour. Makes 6 servings.

Spinach-Cheese Pie

Thaw 4 frozen patty shells in refrigerator about 2 hours. On lightly floured surface roll shells to fit 10-inch pie plate; seal edges together. Let rest 5 minutes. Place in pie plate; flute edges. Cook one 10-ounce package frozen chopped spinach, following package directions; drain well. Combine 6 eggs; one 3-ounce package cream cheese, softened; and ¼ cup shredded sharp American cheese. Beat well. Stir in spinach, 2 tablespoons sliced green onion, 1 tablespoon snipped parsley, ½ teaspoon salt, and dash pepper. Turn into pastry shell; top with 2 tablespoons grated Parmesan cheese. Bake at 425° till edges of filling set, about 15 minutes. Remove from oven; let stand 10 minutes. Serves 8.

Pea and Celery Bake

1 10-ounce package frozen peas
1 bunch celery, bias cut in
   1-inch pieces (4½ cups)
½ cup chopped onion
2 teaspoons instant chicken
   bouillon granules
1 8-ounce can tomato sauce
2 tablespoons margarine *or* butter
½ teaspoon dried oregano, crushed
⅓ cup grated Parmesan cheese

Thaw peas. In saucepan mix celery, onion, bouillon granules, and ½ cup water. Cover; bring to boiling. Reduce heat; simmer till celery is tender, 12 to 15 minutes. Stir in peas, tomato sauce, margarine, and oregano. Bake, uncovered, in 1½-quart casserole at 400° for 30 minutes. Top with cheese. Serves 6 to 8.

Baked Deviled Tomatoes

Halve 4 large tomatoes; place, cut side up, in 13x9x2-inch baking dish. Sprinkle with salt. Spread tops with 1 tablespoon prepared mustard. Mix 2 tablespoons melted butter, 2 tablespoons chopped green pepper, 2 tablespoons chopped celery, and 1 tablespoon chopped green onion. Spoon over tomatoes. Bake at 425° for 8 to 10 minutes. Serves 8.

Nectarine Quick Shortcake

1½ cups packaged biscuit mix
½ cup milk
1 egg
2 tablespoons granulated sugar
½ teaspoon grated lemon peel
2 nectarines
2 tablespoons butter *or* margarine
⅓ cup granulated sugar
2 tablespoons packed brown sugar
½ teaspoon ground cinnamon
    Dairy sour cream

In mixing bowl stir together first 5 ingredients till just moistened. Spread in greased 8x8x2-inch baking pan. Peel and pit nectarines; cut in ¼-inch slices. Arrange slices in rows atop batter. Melt butter; drizzle over fruit. Mix next 3 ingredients; sprinkle over fruit. Bake at 400° for 18 to 20 minutes. Serve warm topped with sour cream. Makes 9 servings.

Fresh Pear Dumplings

A special dessert pictured on pages 38 and 39 —

    Pastry for 2-crust 9-inch pie
6 small pears, peeled and cored
1 3-ounce package cream cheese, softened
2 tablespoons chopped walnuts, toasted
6 teaspoons sugar
1¼ cups sugar
¼ cup red cinnamon candies
2 tablespoons butter *or* margarine

On lightly floured surface roll dough to 21x14-inch rectangle; cut in six 7-inch squares. Place one pear upright on each square. Stir together cheese and nuts. Fill center of each pear with about *1 tablespoon* cheese mixture; sprinkle *1 teaspoon* sugar over each. Moisten edges of pastry with water. Bring corners to center; overlap and pinch edges to seal. Place in 11x7½x1½-inch baking pan.

Cook 1¼ cups sugar, candies, and 1½ cups water till candies dissolve. Bring to boiling; add butter. Pour over dumplings. Bake at 400° for 35 to 40 minutes. Serve warm with light cream, if desired. Makes 6 servings.

Deep Dish Apple Pie

10 cups thinly sliced, peeled apples (about 8 apples)
1 cup sugar
1 cup all-purpose flour
½ teaspoon ground cinnamon
¼ teaspoon ground nutmeg
¼ teaspoon salt
3 tablespoons butter *or* margarine
1 cup all-purpose flour
⅛ teaspoon salt
⅓ cup shortening
    Cold milk
    Sugar
    Light cream

Place apples in 12x7½x2-inch baking dish. Combine next 5 ingredients; mix lightly with apples. Dot with butter. Stir together the 1 cup flour and ⅛ teaspoon salt; cut in shortening till crumbly. Gradually add 2 to 3 tablespoons milk; toss with fork to just dampen. Form ball. On lightly floured surface roll to 13x8½-inch rectangle. Place over fruit; flute edge. Brush with milk; cut steam vents. Sprinkle with sugar. Bake at 400° for 45 to 50 minutes. Serve warm with cream. Serves 8.

Rich Choco-Bread Crumb Pudding

1 6-ounce package semisweet chocolate pieces
1½ cups milk
1 beaten egg
½ cup sugar
¼ teaspoon ground cinnamon
    Dash salt
2½ cups soft bread crumbs
    Light cream

Stir chocolate pieces and *1 cup* of the milk over medium heat till chocolate melts. Remove from heat; stir in remaining milk. Combine with egg, sugar, cinnamon, and salt; beat well. Stir in bread crumbs. Turn into six 6-ounce custard cups. Place cups in 13x9x2-inch baking pan. Add hot water to pan to depth of 1 inch. Bake at 400° till knife inserted off-center comes out clean, 15 to 20 minutes. Serve warm with light cream. Serves 6.

Biscuit Topper

Use this easy-to-make drop biscuit for topping all of the cobbler variations —

- **1 cup all-purpose flour**
- **2 tablespoons granulated sugar**
- **1½ teaspoons baking powder**
- **¼ teaspoon salt**
- **¼ cup butter *or* margarine**
- **1 beaten egg**
- **¼ cup milk**

Thoroughly stir together the flour, sugar, baking powder, and salt. Cut in butter or margarine till mixture is crumbly. Combine the egg and milk; add all at once to the dry ingredients. Stir just to moisten.

Sunshine Cobblers

Use two canned citrus fruits to make this cobbler flavorful and colorful —

- **½ cup packed brown sugar**
- **3 tablespoons all-purpose flour**
- **1 16-ounce can grapefruit-orange sections**
- **1 11-ounce can mandarin orange sections**
- **3 tablespoons butter *or* margarine**

• • •

- **Biscuit Topper**
- **1 tablespoon granulated sugar**
- **⅛ teaspoon ground cinnamon**
- **6 pecan halves**
- **Light cream**

Stir together the brown sugar and flour; gradually blend in a small amount of the juice from the grapefruit-orange sections till smooth. Stir in grapefruit-orange sections with remaining juice and mandarin oranges with juice. Divide mixture among six 10-ounce baking dishes. Dot with butter or margarine. Bake at 425° till mixture is bubbly, 15 to 20 minutes.

Meanwhile, prepare Biscuit Topper and drop into 6 portions atop bubbling hot fruit mixture. Sprinkle with a mixture of granulated sugar and cinnamon. Continue baking at 425° till biscuits are lightly browned, about 20 minutes. Top each with a pecan half. Serve warm with light cream. Makes 6 servings.

Nutty Cherry Cobbler

- **Biscuit Topper**
- **2 tablespoons chopped toasted almonds**
- **1 16-ounce can pitted tart red cherries**
- **½ cup sugar**
- **2 tablespoons quick-cooking tapioca**
- **2 tablespoons butter *or* margarine**
- **Few drops almond extract**
- **1 tablespoon sugar**
- **Vanilla ice cream**

Prepare Biscuit Topper; stir in almonds and set aside. Drain cherries; reserve juice. Add water to juice to make 1½ cups. In saucepan combine fruit, juice, ½ cup sugar, and tapioca; let stand 5 minutes. Cook and stir till thickened, about 5 minutes. Stir in butter or margarine and extract. Turn into 8x1½-inch round baking dish. Drop Biscuit Topper into 6 portions atop bubbling hot fruit. Sprinkle with 1 tablespoon sugar. Bake at 425° till biscuits brown, about 20 minutes. Serve warm with ice cream. Makes 6 servings.

Apple and Raisin Cobbler

- **Biscuit Topper**
- **½ cup packed brown sugar**
- **2 tablespoons cornstarch**
- **¼ teaspoon ground ginger**
- **1¼ cups water**
- **¼ cup raisins**
- **6 cups sliced, peeled apples**
- **1 tablespoon lemon juice**
- **1 tablespoon margarine *or* butter**
- **1 tablespoon granulated sugar**
- **Vanilla ice cream**

Prepare Biscuit Topper and set aside. In saucepan combine the brown sugar, cornstarch, and ginger. Stir in the water and raisins. Cook and stir till thickened. Stir in apples, lemon juice, and margarine. Cook till apples are hot, about 5 minutes. Turn into 2-quart casserole. Drop Biscuit Topper into 8 portions atop bubbling hot fruit. Sprinkle with granulated sugar. Bake at 425° till biscuits are lightly browned, about 20 minutes. Serve warm with vanilla ice cream. Makes 8 servings.

Add variety to easy desserts by making cobblers such as the *Sunshine Cobblers*. The easy Biscuit Topper also is used with the Nutty Cherry, Apple and Raisin, and Fresh Strawberry Cobblers. Try your hand at other variations by using these recipes as guides.

Fresh Strawberry Cobbler

    Biscuit Topper
⅔ **cup sugar**
 2 **tablespoons cornstarch**
1½ **cups water**
 4 **cups fresh *or* frozen strawberries**
 1 **teaspoon vanilla**
 1 **tablespoon sugar**
   Vanilla ice cream

Prepare Biscuit Topper; set aside. In saucepan blend ⅔ cup sugar and cornstarch; stir in water. Cook and stir till thickened and bubbly. Cut any large berries in half. Add berries to mixture in saucepan; cook and stir 5 minutes longer. Stir in vanilla. Turn into 2-quart casserole. Drop Biscuit Topper into 8 portions atop bubbling hot fruit. Sprinkle with 1 tablespoon sugar. Bake at 425° till biscuits are lightly browned, about 25 minutes. Serve warm with ice cream. Makes 8 servings.

Apple-Banana Crunch Pie

 3 **medium apples, peeled, cored, and**
   cut into chunks (3 cups)
 2 **medium bananas, peeled and cut into**
   chunks (2 cups)
 2 **tablespoons lemon juice**
 1 **cup all-purpose flour**
½ **cup granulated sugar**
½ **cup packed brown sugar**
½ **teaspoon ground cinnamon**
½ **teaspoon ground nutmeg**
½ **cup butter *or* margarine, softened**
 1 **unbaked 9-inch pastry shell**

Combine fruits and lemon juice; let stand 10 minutes. Combine flour, sugars, and spices; cut in butter till crumbly. Arrange fruit in pastry shell. Sprinkle with crumb mixture. Bake at 400° for 35 to 40 minutes. Cover top loosely with foil if crumb mixture browns too quickly. Cut in wedges to serve.

Special Oven Cooking

Looking for menus that make use of your microwave, countertop, or roaster oven? Then check in this section. The microwave oven meal on the left includes Beef and Mushroom Loaf, Bean Pot Peppers, and Chocolate Cakelettes. The countertop oven menu on the right features Quiche Monterey, Tomatoes with Herbed Peas, and Fruit Cocktail Cobbler. (See index for page numbers.)

Microwave meals

Cooking with a countertop microwave oven can save time when you're working on a tight schedule. Prepare a whole meal in minutes and reheat leftovers equally fast. This section includes seven microwave dinners that are easy and fun to prepare in this countertop appliance.

FOR SIX WITH EASE

Spareribs Cantonese
Glazed Squash Rings
Tossed Salad   Vinegar and Oil
Sesame-Topped Rolls   Butter
Cran-Apple Compote
Beverage

Preparation tip: Cook the whole squash and compote early in the day. While the ribs cook, slice the squash and finish cooking it while you add garnish to ribs.

Spareribs Cantonese

4 pounds pork spareribs
1 12-ounce jar orange marmalade
    (1 cup)
½ cup soy sauce
½ teaspoon garlic powder
½ teaspoon ground ginger
    Orange slices

Cub ribs in serving-size pieces. Arrange in 12x7½x2-inch glass baking dish. Cover with waxed paper. Cook in countertop microwave oven 10 minutes. Drain off juices and re-arrange ribs in baking dish.

In bowl combine marmalade, soy sauce, garlic powder, ground ginger, ¾ cup water, and dash pepper. Pour mixture over ribs. Cook, uncovered, in countertop microwave oven till done, about 30 minutes.* Occasionally baste and rearrange ribs in dish. Garnish with orange slices. Makes 4 to 6 servings.

Glazed Squash Rings

Place 2 whole acorn squash in countertop microwave oven. Cook till soft, 8 to 10 minutes.* Let stand 5 minutes. Cut in 1-inch slices; discard seeds and ends. Place squash in 12x7½x2-inch glass baking dish. Season with salt and pepper.

In glass measuring cup combine ½ cup maple-flavored syrup and ¼ cup butter. Place in countertop microwave oven and cook 15 *seconds*. Pour over squash. Cover with waxed paper. Cook in countertop microwave oven till heated through, 3 to 5 minutes; baste once. Makes 6 servings.

Cran-Apple Compote

Mix together one 16-ounce can whole cran-berry sauce; 3 cups sliced, peeled apples; and ¼ teaspoon ground ginger. Place in 10x6x2-inch glass baking dish. Cook, uncovered, in countertop microwave oven 2½ minutes; stir. Cook 2½ minutes more; stir. Add one 11-ounce can mandarin orange sections, drained. Cook till apples are tender, about 3 minutes.* Before serving, warm fruit in microwave oven. Top with vanilla ice cream. Serves 6.

✻ *Timings are approximate, as countertop microwave ovens vary by manufacturer. But after trying a few recipes, you will be able to adjust recipe timings to your oven.*

Make quick work of preparing a dinner for six ▶ by serving *Spareribs Cantonese* and *Glazed Squash Rings.* Salad and rolls are the ideal accompaniment to this microwave meal.

SCHOOL DAY LUNCH

Beef and Mushroom Loaf
Bean Pot Peppers
Peach-Cottage Cheese Salad
Hard Rolls   Butter
Radish Roses
Chocolate Cakelettes
Beverage

Preparation tip: *Dovetailing cooking adds time to that already saved by your microwave oven. While the dessert bakes, halve and clean the peppers. While the peppers precook, start making beef loaf. As the beef loaf cooks, make filling for peppers. Bake peppers while loaf rests before you remove it from the baking dish.*

Beef and Mushroom Loaf

This extra fast and taste-tempting recipe is pictured with the menu on pages 88 and 89 —

     1 beaten egg
     3 tablespoons milk
     ¼ cup quick-cooking rolled oats
     1 3-ounce can chopped mushrooms,
          drained
     2 tablespoons snipped parsley
     1 teaspoon onion salt
          • • •
     1 pound ground beef
     ½ cup shredded sharp American cheese

In a bowl combine the beaten egg, milk, rolled oats, chopped mushrooms, parsley, and onion salt; mix well. Add the ground beef; combine thoroughly. Shape ground beef mixture into a 7x1-inch round loaf; place in a 9-inch glass pie plate. Cover with waxed paper and cook in a countertop microwave oven 5 minutes. Remove from oven. Uncover; drain off excess fat. Return to oven. Cook, uncovered, till done, 2 minutes* more.

Top with the shredded cheese. Cook just till cheese melts, about 45 to 60 *seconds*. Let loaf stand 5 minutes before removing from baking dish. Makes 4 servings.

Bean Pot Peppers

     2 large green peppers
       Salt
     1 12-ounce jar baked beans in
          molasses sauce (1½ cups)
     ⅓ cup gingersnap crumbs (5 cookies)
     1 tablespoon instant minced onion
     1 tablespoon packed brown sugar
     2 teaspoons Worcestershire sauce
     1 teaspoon prepared mustard

Halve peppers lengthwise; remove seeds and membranes. Place peppers in a 10x6x2-inch glass baking dish. Cover and cook in a countertop microwave oven 2 minutes. Sprinkle insides of pepper halves with salt. In mixing bowl combine beans, gingersnap crumbs, onion, sugar, Worcestershire sauce, and mustard; mix well. Divide mixture among the four pepper halves. Place in microwave oven. Cook, uncovered, until beans are heated through, about 4 minutes.* Serves 4.

Chocolate Cakelettes

     ⅔ cup all-purpose flour
     ½ cup sugar
     3 tablespoons unsweetened cocoa
          powder
     1 teaspoon baking powder
     ⅛ teaspoon salt
     1 beaten egg
     ⅓ cup water
     ¼ cup cooking oil
     ½ teaspoon vanilla
     ¼ cup semisweet chocolate pieces
       Whipped cream or topping

In a mixing bowl combine the flour, sugar, unsweetened cocoa powder, baking powder, and salt. Stir in the beaten egg, water, cooking oil, and vanilla; mix thoroughly. Stir in the chocolate pieces. Spoon batter into six 6-ounce greased custard cups. Cook 3 at a time, uncovered, in countertop microwave oven till wooden pick comes out clean, about 2 minutes.* Loosen edges of cakes and remove from baking dishes. Serve warm, if desired. Top with whipped cream or whipped topping. Makes 6 cupcakes.

SPEEDY DINNER FOR SIX

Baked Chow Mein
Buttered Broccoli Spears
Sour Cream-Topped Tomatoes
Pumpkin Pudding Cake
Beverage

Preparation tip: *Bake dessert first and cool while you finish the meal. Make chow mein while dessert bakes and then fix the salad while the chow mein bakes.*

Pumpkin Pudding Cake

The pudding starts on the top and sinks to the bottom in this fascinating dessert—

> 1 **cup all-purpose flour**
> ½ **cup granulated sugar**
> ¼ **cup packed brown sugar**
> 2 **teaspoons baking powder**
> 1 **teaspoon pumpkin pie spice**
> ½ **teaspoon salt**
> ½ **cup canned pumpkin**
> ½ **cup milk**
> 2 **tablespoons cooking oil**
> ½ **cup chopped walnuts**
> 1¾ **cups water**
> ¾ **cup packed brown sugar**
> 1 **tablespoon butter *or* margarine**

In a bowl thoroughly combine the flour, granulated sugar, the ¼ cup brown sugar, baking powder, spice, and salt. Add the pumpkin, milk, and oil; stir till smooth. Stir in the nuts. In large glass measuring cup heat water in countertop microwave oven till boiling. Add the ¾ cup brown sugar and butter to boiling water; stir till dissolved. Turn pumpkin mixture into an 8x8x2-inch glass baking dish; spread evenly in dish. Pour boiling water-brown sugar mixture over batter.

Cook, uncovered, in countertop microwave oven until cake has baked appearance, 8 to 9 minutes.* Give pan 4 quarter turns while baking. Serve warm topped with whipped topping, if desired. Makes 6 servings.

Baked Chow Mein

> 1 **pound ground beef**
> ½ **cup chopped onion**
> 1 **16-ounce can chop suey vegetables, drained**
> 1 **10¾-ounce can condensed cream of mushroom soup**
> 1 **3-ounce can sliced mushrooms, drained**
> ½ **cup water**
> 1 **tablespoon soy sauce**
> 1 **3-ounce can chow mein noodles**

In a 10x6x2-inch glass baking dish break up ground beef. Add chopped onion. Cover and cook in countertop microwave oven for 5 minutes, stirring occasionally. Remove from oven; drain off excess fat. Stir in drained chop suey vegetables, mushroom soup, drained mushrooms, water, soy sauce, and *half* of the chow mein noodles; stir till blended. Cook, covered, in microwave oven 6 minutes* longer, stirring occasionally. Sprinkle remaining noodles atop beef mixture. Pass additional soy sauce, if desired. Makes 6 servings.

Sour Cream-Topped Tomatoes

> 3 **medium tomatoes**
> **Salt**
> **Pepper**
> ⅓ **cup dairy sour cream**
> 2 **tablespoons milk**
> 1 **tablespoon snipped parsley**
> ½ **teaspoon prepared horseradish**
> ½ **teaspoon seasoned salt**
> **Lettuce leaves**

Have tomatoes thoroughly chilled. Cut tomatoes in half crosswise. Season with salt and pepper. In bowl stir sour cream and milk together. Stir parsley, horseradish, and seasoned salt into sour cream mixture. Spoon mixture onto tomato halves. Place each tomato half on a lettuce leaf. Makes 6 servings.

✱ *Timings are approximate, as countertop microwave ovens vary by manufacturer. But after trying a few recipes, you will be able to adjust recipe timings to your oven.*

HURRY-UP DINNER FOR TWO

Scallop Stuffing Casseroles *or*
Enchiladas Dos
Baby Limas
Blender Coleslaw *or*
Spinach-Mushroom Salad
Caramel-Pecan Baked Apples
Beverage

Preparation tip: *Bake the dessert first so it can cool slightly before eating. Make main dish while dessert is in oven. Then, bake the main dish and serve the meal.*

Scallop Stuffing Casseroles

Served in individual casseroles —

    8 ounces fresh *or* frozen scallops
    2 tablespoons butter *or* margarine
   ¼ cup herb-seasoned stuffing croutons
   ½ cup chopped onion
    2 tablespoons butter or margarine
    3 tablespoons dry white wine
   ¾ cup herb-seasoned stuffing croutons
    2 beaten eggs
    1 slice Swiss cheese

Thaw frozen scallops. In a 1-cup glass measuring cup melt 1 tablespoon butter in countertop microwave oven, 20 *seconds.* * Add ¼ cup croutons; stir to coat. Set aside.

    In small glass mixing bowl combine onion and 2 tablespoons butter. Cook, uncovered, in microwave oven about 3 minutes. Stir in scallops, wine, 3 tablespoons water, and ¼ teaspoon salt. Cook, covered, in microwave oven till scallops are almost done, about 3 minutes; stir occasionally during cooking. Stir in remaining croutons and eggs; mix well. Spoon into two 1-cup casseroles. Cook, uncovered, till heated through, about 1 minute.

    Top each casserole with half of the buttered croutons. Halve cheese slice diagonally and place a piece on top of each casserole. Heat, uncovered, in microwave oven till cheese melts, about 30 *seconds.* Serves 2.

Enchiladas Dos

   ½ pound lean ground beef
   ¼ cup chopped onion
   ¼ teaspoon salt
    4 tortillas
   ¼ cup canned sauce for tacos
   ½ cup shredded Monterey Jack cheese
      (2 ounces)
    2 tablespoons butter *or* margarine
    3 tablespoons all-purpose flour
    1 teaspoon instant chicken bouillon
      granules
   ½ cup dairy sour cream
    2 tablespoons chopped canned green
      chili peppers

In glass bowl crumble ground beef. Add onion. Cook, uncovered, in countertop microwave oven 2 minutes; stir occasionally to break up meat. Drain. Add salt. Divide meat between the 4 tortillas; top each with *1 tablespoon* of the sauce for tacos and *1 tablespoon* cheese. Roll up. Place, seam side down, in 9-inch glass pie plate. In 2-cup glass measuring cup melt butter in microwave oven 20 *seconds.** Blend in flour. Stir in bouillon granules and 1 cup water. Cook, uncovered, till mixture thickens and bubbles, 2 minutes; stir every 30 *seconds.* Stir moderate amount of hot mixture into sour cream; return to hot mixture. Stir in chili peppers. Pour over tortillas. Sprinkle with remaining cheese. Cook, uncovered, in microwave oven till hot, 3 minutes. Serves 2.

Blender Coleslaw

    Sliced cabbage
   ½ carrot, peeled
   ¼ green pepper, seeded
    1 slice onion
    Coleslaw salad dressing

Fill blender container to 3-cup measure with sliced cabbage. Cut carrot, pepper, and onion in pieces and add to blender. Cover vegetables with cold water. Cover blender and blend at high speed just till vegetables are chopped, about 3 *seconds.* Do not overblend. Drain thoroughly in sieve. Toss with desired amount of bottled coleslaw dressing. Makes 2 servings.

This different way to serve scallops provides a change from the everyday meat and potatoes routine. Serve *Scallop Stuffing Casseroles* in individual casserole dishes. Team with vegetable, salad, and dessert for a delicious meal just for two prepared in a hurry.

Spinach-Mushroom Salad

When fresh spinach is not available, substitute a green leafy vegetable such as lettuce, romaine, or endive, or use a combination for variety —

   1 small clove garlic, halved
   2 cups fresh spinach
   1 hard-cooked egg, sliced
   ½ cup sliced fresh mushrooms
   2 tablespoons salad oil
   1 tablespoon lemon juice
   ¼ teaspoon salt
      Dash freshly ground black pepper

Rub salad bowl with cut garlic clove and discard garlic. Wash spinach thoroughly; dry on paper toweling. Cut away tough stems and tear in bite-size pieces. In bowl combine spinach with sliced egg and mushrooms.

   Shake together the oil, lemon juice, salt, and pepper. Pour over salad before serving; toss lightly. Makes 2 servings.

Caramel-Pecan Baked Apples

   2 large baking apples
   2 teaspoons butter *or* margarine
   2 tablespoons caramel topping
   2 tablespoons chopped pecans

Core apples and peel a strip from the top of each. Place each apple in a 6-ounce custard cup. Fill core of *each* apple with *1 teaspoon* of the butter. Cook, uncovered, in countertop microwave oven 2 minutes. Top *each* apple with *1 tablespoon* caramel topping and *1 tablespoon* chopped nuts. Cook in microwave oven until topping is heated, about 30 *seconds.** Let stand a few minutes until cooled slightly. Makes 2 servings.

✳ *Timings are approximate, as countertop microwave ovens vary by manufacturer. But after trying a few recipes, you will be able to adjust recipe timings to your oven.*

SPECIAL-OCCASION DINNER

Apricot Nectar
Pompano en Papillote
Peas and Water Chestnuts
Wild and Long Grain Rice
Romaine Relish Salad
Brandy-Topped Bananas
Beverage

Preparation tip: *Assemble the fish first and prepare the peas while the fish cooks. Cook the dessert at the same time you're opening the parchment cases on the fish.*

Pompano en Papillote

6 fresh or frozen pompano fillets
2 6½-ounce pouches frozen shrimp
     Newburg, thawed
1 7½-ounce can crab meat, drained,
     flaked, and cartilage removed
1 3-ounce can sliced mushrooms,
     drained
     Dash garlic powder

If fillets are frozen, place in 12x7½x2-inch glass baking dish. Thaw in countertop microwave oven for 2 minutes; 1 minute; 1 minute; then 30 *seconds,** allowing a 2-minute rest period between each thawing time. Separate fillets and set aside.

Meanwhile, cut 6 pieces parchment paper into heart shapes measuring 9 inches long and 5 inches wide (measurements are for parchment heart folded in half). When thawed, place 1 fillet on half of each parchment heart.

In mixing bowl combine Newburg, crab, mushrooms, and garlic powder. Spoon about ⅓ *cup* sauce over each fillet. Fold other half of each parchment heart over fillet to form individual cases. Seal, starting at top of heart, by turning edges up and folding, twisting tip of heart to hold case closed. Place in 12x7½x2-inch glass baking dish. Place in microwave oven; cook 8 minutes. Cut open with large X on each case; fold back. Serves 6.

Peas and Water Chestnuts

Sliced water chestnuts add texture—

3 tablespoons sliced green onion
2 tablespoons butter *or* margarine
2 10-ounce packages frozen peas
1 5-ounce can water chestnuts,
     drained and thinly sliced
¾ teaspoon salt

In a 2-quart glass casserole combine onion and butter. Cover with waxed paper. Cook in countertop microwave oven till onion is tender, about 3 minutes.* Add peas and water chestnuts. Cover with waxed paper and cook in countertop microwave oven till peas are tender, about 8 minutes. Stir occasionally during the last 4 minutes. Add salt; stir in thoroughly. Makes 6 to 8 servings.

Romaine Relish Salad

In small jar combine 1 tablespoon salad oil, 1 tablespoon lemon juice, 1 teaspoon sugar, ½ teaspoon salt, and several dashes ground cinnamon; cover and shake well. Pour over 8 cups torn romaine and one 4-ounce jar pimiento, drained and sliced. Toss lightly to mix. Makes 6 servings.

Brandy-Topped Bananas

Very quick fruit dessert—

¼ cup butter *or* margarine
½ cup packed brown sugar
¼ cup peach *or* apricot brandy
¼ teaspoon ground cinnamon
4 ripe medium bananas
     Vanilla ice cream

In 10x6x2-inch glass baking dish melt butter or margarine in countertop microwave oven, about 30 *seconds.** Stir in brown sugar, brandy, and cinnamon. Peel bananas; cut into ½-inch slices. Stir bananas into brown sugar-butter mixture. Cook, uncovered, in microwave oven 2 minutes, stopping to stir at 45 *seconds* and again at 1½ minutes. Spoon warm banana mixture into dessert dishes and top with ice cream. Makes 6 servings.

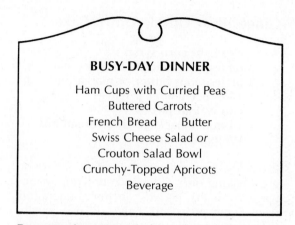

BUSY-DAY DINNER

Ham Cups with Curried Peas
Buttered Carrots
French Bread   Butter
Swiss Cheese Salad *or*
Crouton Salad Bowl
Crunchy-Topped Apricots
Beverage

Preparation tip: *If the salad you choose needs chilling, make it ahead of time. Bake the ham cups and then the dessert. Make the creamed peas last and spoon into ham cups.*

Swiss Cheese Salad

- **1 ounce Swiss cheese, cut in narrow strips**
- **1 hard-cooked egg, chopped**
- **3 tablespoons chopped celery**
- **2 tablespoons chopped green pepper**
- **1 teaspoon chopped green onion**
- **3 tablespoons mayonnaise *or* salad dressing**
- **1 teaspoon vinegar**
- **½ teaspoon prepared mustard**
  Salt
- **1 small tomato, sliced**
  Lettuce leaves

Combine cheese, egg, celery, green pepper, and onion. Combine mayonnaise, vinegar, and mustard; season to taste with salt. Toss with cheese mixture. Chill. Serve on tomato slices on lettuce leaf. Makes 2 servings.

Crouton Salad Bowl

- **1 small head Boston lettuce**
- **¼ cup herb-seasoned croutons**
  Caesar salad dressing

Tear lettuce in bite-size pieces into a salad bowl. Add croutons and top with salad dressing. Toss lightly to mix. Makes 2 servings.

Ham Cups with Curried Peas

- **1 beaten egg**
- **2 tablespoons milk**
- **¾ cup soft bread crumbs (1 slice)**
- **3 tablespoons finely chopped onion**
- **½ teaspoon dry mustard**
- **½ pound ground fully cooked ham**
- **1 tablespoon butter *or* margarine**
- **½ teaspoon curry powder**
- **1 tablespoon all-purpose flour**
- **⅛ teaspoon salt**
  Dash pepper
- **⅔ cup milk**
- **1 8½-ounce can peas, drained**

Combine egg, 2 tablespoons milk, bread crumbs, onion, and mustard; add ham and mix well. Shape mixture into two 4-inch patties; fit each into a 6-ounce custard cup. Cook, uncovered, in countertop microwave oven till meat is done, about 4 minutes.* Remove from oven; keep warm. In 2-cup glass measuring cup heat butter and curry in microwave oven till butter melts, about 20 *seconds*. Blend in flour, salt, and pepper. Stir in ⅔ cup milk. Cook in microwave oven till mixture thickens, about 2 minutes; stir every 30 *seconds*. Stir in peas. Cook in microwave oven till heated through, about 30 *seconds*. Lift baked ham cups from custard cups to serving plate; fill with creamed peas. Makes 2 servings.

Crunchy-Topped Apricots

Drain one 8¾-ounce can unpeeled apricot halves; divide apricots between two 6-ounce custard cups. Combine 2 tablespoons packed brown sugar, 2 tablespoons quick-cooking rolled oats, 1 tablespoon all-purpose flour, and dash ground nutmeg. Cut 1 tablespoon butter into brown sugar mixture till crumbly. Sprinkle crumbly mixture over apricots. Cook in countertop microwave oven till fruit is heated through, about 2 minutes.* Serve warm with vanilla ice cream. Makes 2 servings.

✳ *Timings are approximate, as countertop microwave ovens vary by manufacturer. But after trying a few recipes, you will be able to adjust recipe timings to your oven.*

INDOOR BARBECUE

Barbecued Chicken
New Potatoes
Buttered Asparagus Spears
Boston Cottage Cheese Toss
Ginger-Pear Upside-Down Cake
Beverage

Preparation tip: *Make the dessert while the chicken bakes. Bake the dessert and toss the salad. Let the dessert cool slightly while you're eating the rest of the meal.*

Barbecued Chicken

An indoor barbecue dinner made in a hurry with the microwave oven—

> 1 2- to 2½-pound ready-to-cook
>   broiler-fryer chicken, cut up
> • • •
> 2 tablespoons butter *or* margarine
> ½ cup chopped onion
> ¼ cup chopped celery
> • • •
> 1 cup canned whole cranberry sauce
> ½ cup catsup
> 2 tablespoons lemon juice
> 1 tablespoon packed brown sugar
> 1 tablespoon Worcestershire sauce
> 1 tablespoon prepared mustard
> 1 tablespoon vinegar

Cut chicken in uniformly sized pieces; set aside. Melt butter in 12x7½x2-inch glass baking dish in countertop microwave oven, about 30 *seconds*.* Stir in chopped onion and celery. Cook in microwave oven 3 minutes. Stir in the cranberry sauce, catsup, lemon juice, brown sugar, Worcestershire sauce, mustard, and vinegar. Place chicken pieces in the baking dish; coat with sauce. Cover with waxed paper. Cook in microwave oven 15 minutes, turning dish once for even cooking. Turn chicken and cook, uncovered, in microwave oven 5 minutes more, spooning sauce over occasionally. Makes 4 servings.

Ginger-Pear Upside-Down Cake

> ¼ cup light corn syrup
> 3 tablespoons packed brown sugar
> 2 tablespoons butter *or* margarine
> 1 16-ounce can pear halves
> ⅓ cup walnut pieces
> 1 14-ounce package gingerbread mix
>   Whipped cream

Place first 3 ingredients in 8 x 1½-inch round glass baking dish. Cook in countertop microwave oven 20 *seconds*.* to melt butter; mix well. Drain pears; cut halves in two lengthwise. Place nut piece in each quarter. Arrange in dish spoke-fashion, cut side down. Place remaining nuts in center of baking dish. Prepare gingerbread mix, following package directions. Pour *1½ cups* batter over pears and nuts; smooth surface. Cook, uncovered, in microwave oven till wooden pick comes out clean, 7 to 8 minutes. Let stand 1 minute; loosen edge and invert onto serving plate. Serve with whipped cream. Serves 6 to 8.
   Note: With extra batter fill paper bake cup-lined 6-ounce custard cups ½ full. Bake in microwave oven, 3 at a time, for 45 *seconds*.

Boston Cottage Cheese Toss

In large bowl sprinkle 6 cups torn Boston or Bibb lettuce with salt and pepper. Mix 1 tablespoon salad oil and 1 tablespoon wine vinegar; toss with lettuce. Add 1 cup small curd cream-style cottage cheese; 1 medium avocado, peeled and diced; 1 medium dill pickle, coarsely chopped; and 2 tablespoons sliced green onion. Toss lightly. Garnish with 2 sliced hard-cooked eggs. Serves 4.

✳ *Timings are approximate, as countertop microwave ovens vary by manufacturer. But after trying a few recipes, you will be able to adjust recipe timings to your oven.*

Easy-to-make *Ginger-Pear Upside-Down Cake* ▶ ends the ordinary meal in out-of-the-ordinary style. Dollops of whipped cream top the convenience mix dessert.

Countertop oven recipes

You'll find that you can use even the smallest countertop oven for a variety of cooking tasks. Make best use of the oven by experimenting with various containers and by referring to the use-and-care booklet.

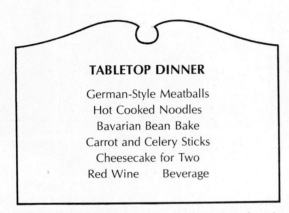

TABLETOP DINNER

German-Style Meatballs
Hot Cooked Noodles
Bavarian Bean Bake
Carrot and Celery Sticks
Cheesecake for Two
Red Wine   Beverage

Preparation tip: Make cheesecake ahead. Prepare meatballs and bake 1 hour. Add green beans 35 minutes before meat is done.

Bavarian Bean Bake

    1 8-ounce can French-style green
       beans, drained
    ½ small apple, cored and sliced
    1 teaspoon butter *or* margarine

In a 10-ounce baking dish combine beans and apple. Dot with butter. Bake, covered, in countertop oven at 375° till apples are tender, about 35 minutes.* Makes 2 servings.

Cheesecake for Two

Combine ¼ cup finely crushed graham crackers, 1 tablespoon melted butter, and 1 teaspoon sugar. Press into 5x5x1½-inch baking dish. In small mixing bowl beat together one 3-ounce package cream cheese, softened; 1 egg; ¼ cup sugar; and 1 teaspoon lemon juice. Pour into crust. Bake in countertop oven at 350° till filling is firm, 20 to 25 minutes.* Top with cherry preserves. Makes 2 servings.

German-Style Meatballs

Subtly flavored with ginger —

    2 tablespoons chopped onion
    1 teaspoon butter *or* margarine
    ¾ cup soft bread crumbs (1 slice)
    1 tablespoon milk
    ½ teaspoon prepared mustard
    ½ pound ground beef
        • • •
    1 2-ounce can chopped mushrooms,
       drained
    2 gingersnap cookies, coarsely
       crushed
    1 tablespoon packed brown sugar
    ½ teaspoon instant beef bouillon
       granules

Cook onion in butter till tender but not brown. In mixing bowl combine cooked onion, bread crumbs, milk, mustard, ½ teaspoon salt, and dash pepper; add beef and mix well. Shape mixture into 6 meatballs. Place in 3-cup casserole. In saucepan combine mushrooms, gingersnap crumbs, brown sugar, bouillon granules, and ½ cup water. Cook and stir over medium heat till mixture thickens and bubbles. Pour over meatballs. Cover and bake in countertop oven at 375° till meatballs are cooked through, about 1 hour.* Serves 2.

✱ *Timings for these recipes are approximate, as countertop ovens vary by manufacturer. But after trying a few recipes, you will be able to adjust recipe timings to your oven.*

German-Style Meatballs boast a robust sauce ▶ of beef bouillon, gingersnaps, and mushrooms. For variety, creamy *Cheesecake for Two* can team up with any flavor of preserves.

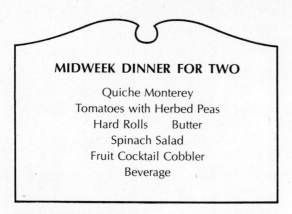

MIDWEEK DINNER FOR TWO

Quiche Monterey
Tomatoes with Herbed Peas
Hard Rolls   Butter
Spinach Salad
Fruit Cocktail Cobbler
Beverage

Preparation tip: *Bake the cobbler, then let stand on a cooling rack. Prepare the quiche and tomatoes. Bake the quiche, then bake the tomatoes 25 minutes before serving. Serve quiche and tomatoes together.*

Quiche Monterey

A cheese and bacon-flavored quiche shown on pages 88 and 89 —

Pastry Shell
• • •
1 beaten egg
½ cup shredded Monterey Jack cheese
   (2 ounces)
⅓ cup milk
4 slices bacon, crisp-cooked, drained,
   and crumbled

Prepare Pastry Shell. Bake pastry shell in countertop oven at 375° for 10 minutes.* In small mixing bowl combine egg, cheese, milk, and bacon. Turn into partially baked pastry shell. Bake in countertop oven at 375° till knife inserted halfway between center and edge comes out clean, 35 to 40 minutes. Let stand 5 minutes before serving. Makes 2 servings.

Pastry Shell: Stir together ½ cup all-purpose flour and ¼ teaspoon salt; cut in 3 tablespoons shortening till mixture resembles coarse crumbs. Sprinkle with 1 tablespoon of cold water. Gently toss with a fork and push moistened part to one side. Repeat with ½ tablespoon more water if needed. Gather up mixture with fingers; form into a ball. On lightly floured surface flatten dough slightly; roll to an 8-inch circle. Fit into a 6-inch fluted baking dish. Turn under; flute edge. *Do not prick.*

Tomatoes with Herbed Peas

A delicious way to use leftover peas. Next time, try this one substituting mixed vegetables —

2 small tomatoes
   Salt
   Pepper
⅓ cup cooked peas
½ teaspoon instant minced onion
¼ teaspoon dried rosemary, crushed
   Butter *or* margarine

Cut a thin slice from the top of each tomato. Hollow out slightly. Sprinkle insides lightly with salt and pepper. Place the tomatoes in two 6-ounce baking dishes. Combine next 3 ingredients. Spoon into center of each tomato. Bake in countertop oven at 375° till peas are heated through, about 25 minutes.* Before serving, top with butter. Makes 2 servings.

Fruit Cocktail Cobbler

Orange peel and juice are outstanding flavor ingredients in this oven dessert —

⅓ cup all-purpose flour
2 tablespoons sugar
½ teaspoon baking powder
   Dash salt
2 tablespoons butter *or* margarine
1 tablespoon milk
2 tablespoons chopped pecans
¼ teaspoon shredded orange peel
• • •
1 8¾-ounce can fruit cocktail
1 tablespoon butter *or* margarine
2 teaspoons cornstarch
1 tablespoon orange juice

For biscuit topping stir together the flour, sugar, baking powder, and salt. Cut in the 2 tablespoons butter till crumbly. Stir in the milk, pecans, and orange peel just till moistened. Set aside. In a small saucepan combine undrained fruit cocktail, the 1 tablespoon butter, and cornstarch. Cook and stir over moderate heat till thickened and bubbly. Stir in orange juice. Pour into a 20-ounce baking dish. Drop biscuit topping in 2 portions atop bubbling hot fruit. Bake in countertop oven at 375° till biscuits are golden, about 35 minutes.* Serves 2.

EASY TOASTER OVEN DINNER

Sausage Spoon Bread
Baked Peas Deluxe
Breadsticks
Honey-Dressed Citrus Salad
Toasted Almond Custards
Beverage

Preparation tip: *Assemble the fruit and dressing, then chill. Make and bake the custards, then let them cool on a rack while preparing the rest of the meal. Make and bake the spoon bread. After the first 15 minutes of baking time add peas to the countertop oven.*

Baked Peas Deluxe

    1 8½-ounce can peas, drained
    1 tablespoon sweet French salad
        dressing
    1 tablespoon finely chopped celery

In a 10-ounce deep pie dish combine the peas, salad dressing, chopped celery, dash salt, and dash pepper. Bake, covered, in countertop oven at 350° till peas are heated through, about 20 minutes.* Serves 2.

Honey-Dressed Citrus Salad

    2 tablespoons mayonnaise
    2 teaspoons honey
    ⅛ teaspoon celery seed
        Dash paprika
        Dash salt
    1 8-ounce can orange and grapefruit
        sections, drained
        Lettuce
    1 tablespoon raisins

In small mixing bowl combine mayonnaise, honey, celery seed, paprika, and dash salt. Chill. Arrange fruit sections on 2 lettuce-lined salad plates. Sprinkle raisins atop fruit. Before serving, spoon dressing atop fruit. Serves 2.

Sausage Spoon Bread

Plan on serving two delicious and generous portions from this pork and corn casserole—

    ¼ cup all-purpose flour
    ¼ cup yellow cornmeal
    1 teaspoon sugar
    ½ teaspoon baking powder
        • • •
    1 beaten egg
    1 8-ounce can cream-style corn
    4 ounces bulk pork sausage, cooked
        and drained
    ¼ cup shredded Swiss cheese

In a mixing bowl combine the flour, cornmeal, sugar, and baking powder. Stir in the beaten egg, cream-style corn, and cooked sausage. Turn the mixture into a 15-ounce baking dish. Bake, uncovered, in countertop oven at 350° for 30 minutes.* Sprinkle with the shredded Swiss cheese. Bake till knife inserted halfway between center and edge comes out clean, 5 minutes more. Makes 2 servings.

Toasted Almond Custards

Doubly good with the flavor of almond baked in the custard and nuts sprinkled atop—

    1 slightly beaten egg
    2 tablespoons sugar
    ⅛ teaspoon almond extract
        Dash salt
    ¾ cup milk
        • • •
    1 tablespoon toasted chopped almonds

In a mixing bowl combine the beaten egg, sugar, almond extract, and salt. Mix well. Gradually stir in milk. Pour custard mixture into two 6-ounce custard cups. Bake custards in countertop oven at 350° till a knife inserted just off-center comes out clean, about 20 minutes. Remove from oven. Sprinkle custards with toasted chopped almonds and serve warm. Makes 2 servings.

❋ *Timings for these recipes are approximate, as countertop ovens vary by manufacturer. But after trying a few recipes, you will be able to adjust recipe timings to your oven.*

SATURDAY NIGHT SUPPER

Fiesta Salmon
Zucchini-Tomato Combo
Tortillas
Avocado and Orange Sections
Pudding and Puffs
Beverage

Preparation tip: Bake the meringue shells early in the day so they can cool.

Fiesta Salmon

½ of an 11-ounce can condensed
    Cheddar cheese soup
3 tablespoons milk
3 tablespoons chopped canned green
    chili peppers
2 teaspoons instant minced onion
1 7¾-ounce can salmon *or* 1 6½- or 7-
    ounce can tuna, drained and
    broken into chunks
¾ cup coarsely crushed tortilla chips

In a saucepan combine soup, milk, chili peppers, and onion. Heat and stir till bubbly. Add salmon or tuna and ½ *cup* of the corn chips. Turn mixture into two 1-cup casseroles. Top with remaining corn chips. Bake in countertop oven at 375° till heated through, about 30 minutes.* Makes 2 servings.

Zucchini-Tomato Combo

1 small zucchini, sliced (¾ cup)
1 small tomato, peeled, seeded, and
    chopped
½ teaspoon lemon juice
¼ teaspoon celery flakes

Cook zucchini in boiling salted water for 5 minutes; drain well. Combine with remaining ingredients, ⅛ teaspoon salt, and dash pepper in 1½-cup casserole. Bake, covered, in countertop oven at 375° for 30 minutes.* Serves 2.

Pudding and Puffs

Keep the two extra meringues in the freezer to enjoy later with either of the toppers—

1 egg white
¼ teaspoon cream of tartar
¼ teaspoon vanilla
⅓ cup sugar
• • •
½ cup toffee ice cream
    Mocha-Mallow Topper *or*
    Banana Pudding Topper

Have egg white at room temperature. Add cream of tartar, vanilla, and dash salt; beat to soft peaks. Gradually add sugar, beating till very stiff peaks form and sugar is dissolved. Cut foil to fit countertop oven baking pan; draw four 3-inch diameter circles. Shape ¼ of the meringue into a shell on each circle. Place foil on insert pan. Bake in oven at 300° for 40 minutes.* Turn off heat and let meringues dry in oven (door closed) 40 minutes longer. Remove from foil and cool meringue shells to room temperature. Freeze 2 shells for later use.

Place each of remaining shells on a plate. Scoop ¼ cup of the ice cream into each shell and top with Mocha-Mallow Topper or Banana Pudding Topper. Makes 2 servings.

Mocha-Mallow Topper: Combine one 5-ounce can chocolate pudding, ¼ cup tiny marshmallows, and 2 tablespoons coffee liqueur *or* prepared coffee.

Banana Pudding Topper: Combine one 5-ounce can banana pudding and 1 tablespoon milk. Slice one small banana and place some of the banana on each meringue shell. Top each meringue shell with toffee ice cream, remaining banana slices, and pudding.

✳ *Timings for these recipes are approximate, as countertop ovens vary by manufacturer. But after trying a few recipes, you will be able to adjust recipe timings to your oven.*

Entertain a special guest when *Fiesta Salmon* ▶ is the main course accompanied by zippy *Succhini-Tomato Combo*. Present a dessert with flair—serve rich yet refreshing *Pudding and Puffs* with either of the pudding toppers.

DINNER FOR ONE

Beef and Bacon Loaf
Zucchini Parmigiana
Italian Bread   Butter
Green Salad   Italian Dressing
Doughnut Sundae
Beverage

Preparation tip: *Assemble the meat loaf and the zucchini casserole. Both dishes can be prepared in a short time. Bake together in the countertop oven for 30 minutes. Sprinkle the cheese on the zucchini and melt it in the oven during the additional 5 minutes of baking. Assemble the dessert just before serving, since this only takes a few minutes to prepare.*

Cooking for one

Throw out the idea that cooking for one is tedious. Make it an adventure—and save both time and money.

Plan menus for a week or longer, and allow for leftovers to use in future meals. Make up a market list, shop, and set aside time for cooking.

Buy in quantity those items you'll use often—ground meat, poultry, canned vegetables, and fruits—and in small amounts those items you'll use rarely. Sometimes, small cans are the best buy because of less waste.

You can save time by cooking for more than one meal at a time. Prepare a large dish—chicken, meatballs, beef stew—and divide into several individual portions for use later as three or four meals.

Using small baking dishes, you can have a week's supply of meals ready for the freezer in a few hours. Not only do you save freezer space, but you can vary the size of the portions to satisfy your appetite, thus eliminating wasted food.

Then, at mealtime, all you need to do is place the frozen food portion in the oven and heat up some vegetables—while you read the paper.

Beef and Bacon Loaf

Leftovers make a tasty lunchbox sandwich—

1 beaten egg
2 tablespoons milk
2 slices bacon, crisp-cooked, drained, and crumbled
½ cup soft bread crumbs
⅛ teaspoon garlic salt
Dash pepper
• • •
½ pound lean ground beef

In a mixing bowl combine the egg, milk, cooked bacon, bread crumbs, garlic salt, and pepper. Add the ground beef and mix well. Place meat loaf mixture in a 4½x2½x1½-inch loaf pan. Bake in countertop oven at 350° till done, about 35 minutes. Drain off any excess fat, if necessary. Makes 1 serving.

Zucchini Parmigiana

1 small zucchini, sliced
¼ cup tomato sauce
Dash dried basil, crushed
Dash salt
Dash pepper
¼ cup shredded mozzarella cheese

Place *half* of the zucchini slices in a 1-cup baking dish. Combine tomato sauce, basil, salt, and pepper. Spoon *half* the sauce over zucchini. Top with *half* the cheese. Top with remaining zucchini and sauce. Bake, covered, in countertop oven at 350° till zucchini is heated through, about 30 minutes. Top with remaining cheese and bake till cheese melts, 3 to 5 minutes longer. Makes 1 serving.

Doughnut Sundae

1 plain cake *or* raised doughnut
1 tablespoon crunchy peanut butter
Vanilla ice cream
2 tablespoons fudge sauce

Spread top of doughnut with peanut butter. Place a scoop of ice cream in center of doughnut. Top with sauce. Makes 1 serving.

Preparation tip: *Make and freeze the salad ahead of time. Assemble the main dish, vegetable casserole, and dessert in roaster oven baking dishes, and bake them together in the roaster oven for 1 hour and 40 minutes.*

Smoky Barbecued Chicken

  1 2½- to 3-pound ready-to-cook broiler-
     fryer chicken, cut up
¼ cup cooking oil
½ cup bottled smoke-flavor barbecue
     sauce
  2 tablespoons all-purpose flour
  2 tablespoons honey
½ teaspoon dried basil, crushed

In skillet brown the chicken in hot oil; drain off excess fat. Transfer chicken to 2-quart glass roaster dish. Combine remaining ingredients. Brush over chicken. Bake, uncovered, in roaster oven at 350° till done, 1 hour and 40 minutes. Remove chicken. Skim fat from sauce; serve with chicken. Serves 4.

Potato and Vegetable Scallop

In 7-cup glass roaster dish place 2 cups sliced raw potatoes and one 10-ounce package frozen mixed vegetables, thawed. Combine one 10¾-ounce can condensed cream of celery soup, 2 tablespoons chopped onion, ½ teaspoon salt, and dash bottled hot pepper sauce; pour over all. Bake, covered, in roaster oven at 350° till potatoes are tender and vegetables are heated through, about 1 hour and 40 minutes. Sprinkle with paprika. Makes 4 servings.

Frozen Peachy Salad

A change-of-pace salad made creamy with pineapple yogurt and cream cheese —

  1 8¾-ounce can peach slices
  1 8¾-ounce can pitted dark sweet
     cherries, drained
  1 cup tiny marshmallows
  1 3-ounce package cream cheese
  2 tablespoons sugar
⅛ teaspoon salt
  1 8-ounce carton pineapple yogurt
    Lettuce

Drain peach slices; reserve ¼ cup syrup. Cut up peach slices and cherries. In a small saucepan combine reserved peach syrup with marshmallows. Stir over low heat till marshmallows melt. Cool slightly.

In a mixing bowl beat cream cheese until smooth. Add sugar and salt; beat till fluffy. Stir in marshmallow mixture and yogurt; mix till smooth. Stir in cherries and peaches. Turn mixture into paper bake cup-lined muffin pans and freeze the salad till firm. Remove from freezer and place salad in refrigerator section 15 minutes before serving. Peel off the paper bake cups and serve the individual salads on lettuce. Makes 6 servings.

Minted Fruit Compote

Whipped cream enriches this hot fruit compote, which is 'cooled' with mint liqueur —

  1 13¼-ounce can pineapple tidbits
  1 11-ounce can mandarin orange
     sections, drained
  2 tablespoons white crème de menthe
½ cup whipping cream
  2 tablespoons sugar
  4 red *or* green maraschino cherries

In 7-cup glass roaster dish combine undrained pineapple, orange sections, and crème de menthe. Bake, covered, in roaster oven at 350° for 1 hour and 40 minutes. Let stand at room temperature till ready to serve. Beat whipping cream with sugar till stiff peaks form and sugar is dissolved. Before serving, garnish fruit with a dollop of whipped cream; top with a red or green maraschino cherry. Makes 4 servings.

INDEX

A-B

G-O

P-R